KV-012-200

R32010

© ASSOULINE, 1998
26 rue Danielle Casanova
75002 Paris (France)
http://www.imaginet.fr/assouline
Tel: +33 1 42 60 33 84
Fax: +33 1 42 60 33 85

First published in Italy by Editions Assouline, 1998
A Noir

Distributed to the U.S. trade by St. Martin's Press, New York
Distributed in Canada by McLelland & Stewart
Distributed in all other countries by Thames and Hudson
(Distributors) Ltd., London

All rights reserved. No part of this publication may be reproduced,
stored in a retrieval system, or transmitted in any form or by any
means, electronic, mechanical, photocopying, recording, or
otherwise, without prior consent of the publishers.

ISBN: 2 84323 068 3

Translated from the Italian by Francesca Havens
Typesetting: Claire Stevens
Photoengraving: F.lli Colombo Fotolito Milano (Italy)
Printed and bound by G. Canale & Co. (Italy)

A NOIR

project director: **FRANCA SOZZANI**
art director: **LUCA STOPPINI**
editors: **MARIUCCIA CASADIO**
PASQUALE LECCESE

"A, NOIR CORSET VELU DES MOUCHES ÉCLATANTES/ QUI BOMBINENT AUTOUR DES PUANTEURS CRUELLES, / GOLFES D'OMBRE...

"les voyelles" - arthur rimbaud

A SHORT GLOSSARY OF BLACK
By Mariuccia Casadio

A NOIR The title of the book. *A Noir*, is the beginning of the first verse of the poem *Les Voyelles* by Arthur Rimbaud. Rimbaud goes on to propose the following intriguing metaphor for the colour black: '*A noir, corset velu des mouches éclatantes / Qui bombinent autour de puanteurs cruelles, / Golfes d'ombre ...*' ('A. Black, hairy corset of blatant flies / Splurging around cruel stenches / Gulfs of darkness ... ').
Besides pointing us back to the late nineteenth century, when by debatable coincidence black was the dominant colour in bourgeois clothing styles, the connection to Rimbaud is also a link to the French 'accursed poetry' of the time. The dark and gloomy mood of a collection he later baptized *A Season in Hell* comes across clearly in the reckless, restless, violently passionate, nihilistic verses he creates, full of a sense of their own futility. It is no mistake that this little poem associates the colour black with the first letter of the alphabet, the minimum level of expression. Black can be either the most minimal of colours or the king of colours: in Rimbaud's verse the most extreme aspects of an endless spectrum of varying hues make their presence felt. Black becomes the infinite source of metaphor. '*Corset velu des mouches éclatantes*' is a disturbingly rich metaphor. '*Qui bombinent autour de puanteurs cruelles*' is an image conveying the pain and danger inherent in the nature of things and feelings. '*Golfes d'ombre*' suggests that black is feminine. Rimbaud's black, an aesthetic, erotic, sexual, seductive colour with the power to attract and repel simultaneously, is quite contemporary. It is in perfect harmony with the art and fashion worlds of today. With creators such as Rebecca Horn and Marlene Dumas, Damien Hirst and Matthew Barney, Rei Kawakubo and Alexander McQueen, not to mention Diane Arbus and Helmut Newton, *A Noir* is making its contribution to this endless stream of allusion.

AZZEDINE ALAÏA (Tunisia, in Paris since 1957). Fashion designer. Established in Paris where he opened his own studio (first show in 1982) after working for Dior, Laroche and Mugler. He promotes the liberation of women through extremely feminine and sexy clothing. Little big man of haute couture, the image that springs to mind is of him, dressed in oriental-style black outfits, surrounded by his tremendously tall, elongated models as they try on his figure-hugging outfits. Few designers have such an innate sense of harmony and beauty.

AMBIGUITY n. To be ambiguous, unclear. From Latin *ambigere* 'push something in two directions'. It is black's ambiguous nature that has ensured it success and longevity in art and fashion. Its ambiguity is expressed through ambivalent visual effects (*q.v.* Ambivalence). For instance: superficiality versus depth; inconsistency versus consistency; empty versus full; light versus liquid; signs versus tears, etc.

AMBIVALENCE n. The simultaneous presence of contradictory emotions or feelings towards the same person or thing. A term used in psychoanalysis in relation to split personalities, a vein of ambivalence runs through art seen as a metaphor for splits with nature, culture, the self, one's own art, etc. This bipolarity, this contrast or otherness, is expressed most visibly in the play between black and white. (*q.v.* B/W).

ANNUL – ANNULMENT 1. v. t. 2. n. To frustrate, annihilate, destroy. The consequences of taking away value, authority or meaning from something. The presence of black in art, ideology, costume and fashion has always meant a radical attempt to destroy. To wipe out physicality, or undermine a position of power or dominance, or eradicate technical virtuousity. Or it can be a dignified artistic statement about an impeccably homogeneous surface, a mirror, a blackboard, or a dialectical breakthrough. With artists like Reinhardt and Kosuth, Morris and Bourgeois, many ethical implications and new aesthetic identities have arisen from this process of annulment.

ANTAGONIST n. Said of things and people who are in competition with others. Every struggle involving space and colour, or ethics and the visual, that black manages to interweave with other meanings usually ends with black in conflict with the rest. The perception we have of the presence of black in the image is immediate and unequivocal. It makes itself into a priority.

ANTI Prefix used in compound words with meanings like hostility, aversion, contrast, reversal, etc. Antithetical, antiestablishment, anti-government, anti-nuclear – black generally has a strong predisposition to be anti everything. It was 'in' in 1968 and 1977; punk and new wave; minimalism and maximalism; existentialism and decadentism; 'accursed' poetry and the beat generation, etc.

ANTICIPATORY a. To appear ahead of a particular historical epoch or a period in fashion, but also to speed up the appearance of something, to arrive earlier than anticipated.

ANTIDOTE n. In reference to the colour black, the capacity to neutralize formal, chromatic and environmental interference and to efface or mask perception of random visual structures. It can therefore be seen as an antidote to redundancy, to chaos and the uncontrollable stratification of aesthetic information.

ANTIQUITY n. Refers to objects and institutions from the past, or which show obvious signs of wear or decay. Also: upholder of an old order, of the aesthetics of the pre-electric era Hostile to Western culture owing to the aesthetic damage caused by the birth of modernism, Yunichiro Tanizaki closes his *In Praise of Shadows* with an illuminating eulogy of the past: ''... I would push back into the shadows the things that come forward too clearly, I would strip away the useless decoration. I do not ask that this be done everywhere, but perhaps we may be allowed at least one mansion where we can turn off the electric lights and see what it is like without them.' (Leete's Island Books, USA, 1977, p. 42).

ANTITHETICAL a. That which is in antithesis or direct contrast (*q.v.* Anti).

MICHELANGELO ANTONIONI (Ferrara, 1912). Cinema director. With his luminous intellect and unforgettable iconographical talent, he has portrayed Italian society since the Second World War, from neorealism through to alienation. Most widely recognized films: *Cronica di un amore*, *Il Grido*, *Deserto Rosso* and *Blow Up*. They are all frescos of an awkwardness in individuals, an inability to communicate, of failed quests for erotic or amorous encounters. He is advocate of an interesting theory according to which every mood has a corresponding colour. Needless to say, the main body of his expression is black. Or, a total saturation of light, if we consider it as an intense, existentialist metaphor for the endless wait. Antonioni's films could be regarded as gaps of light breaking into the darkness and silence. The subject of every film corresponds to a different colour, generating a great tonal cycle from black to white and back again to black.

ART Art derived from the conceptual use of black as negation and effacement leads us to various interpretations of the present, whether existentialist, narrative, synthetic, emphatic or autobiographical. From its use as a monochromatic choice of how to proceed, unaltered in time, to the black of action and encounter that assaults the page with its inescapably incisive, structural and/or descriptive capacities, this colour by itself accounts for the most radical chapters in twentieth-century avant-garde and neo-avant-garde art. The only colour that can compete with black in terms of visual effectiveness and its capacity to cross barriers, is white. It is in black and white that the following artists make their appearance and state their identities: Ad Reinhardt, Francesco Lo Savio, Piero Manzoni, Robert Morris, Jannis Kounellis, Sol LeWitt, Joseph Kosuth, Rebecca Horn, Louise Bourgeois, Robert Rauschenberg, Giulio Paolini, etc. (see also Mariuccia Casadio's essay, p. 58–61).

ANTONIN ARTAUD (1896–1948). French writer, actor and stage director. His theoretical work includes two manifestos entitled *Theatre of Cruelty* (1932) which form the basis of his celebrated collection of essays *The Theatre and Its Double* (1938), in which words are sacrificed to gestures and the theatre is seen as a continuation, rather than an illustration, of life. Famous for his contribution to Late Gothic literature, he translated Gregory Matthew Lewis' masterpiece *The Monk* (1796). Frequent allusions are made in homage to both the man and to his creations in contemporary art and narrative, for instance in the work of Alberto Savinio and Julian Schnabel. His creations include *Eliogabal, ou l'anarchiste couronné* (1934), and his self-portrait, which has become an immediately recognisable icon.

RICHARD AVEDON (New York, 1923). Photographer. Hired in 1945 by Brodovitch, art director of *Harper's Bazaar*, to photograph personalities in the fashion world. Twenty years later he started to collaborate with *Vogue*, alongside Diana Vreeland. Famous for his original interpretations of fashion as well as his portraiture, Avedon is equally known for his use of wide-angled lenses, unexpected angles and the stroboscopic lights he uses to capture unusual and deforming expressions that often seem divorced from the faces of his subjects. Before dedicating himself to the studio work he is known for today, he carried out fashion assignments choosing locations like zoos and circuses, NASA launch sites at Cape Canaveral and urban rubbish dumps, encouraging his models to move with the greatest detachment and naturalness.

B/W (Black and White). A technique in photography and cinematography, but also a reference to conceptual expressions of representative form, such as the theory of perception, among others. In photography, black and white is synonymous with reportage, with images linked to fashion, and with subjects where photography is being used to create art. Its representatives range from Cartier–Bresson to Giacomelli, Robert Frank to Mapplethorpe. In art we are reminded of movements like the Optical movement or Art Brut (Vasarely to Dubuffet), or the Bauhaus movement (for example the artist Joseph Albers) with its important contribution to the the psychology of perception, the Russian Avant-garde (Malevich to Delaunay), the U.S. Minimalist movement (Sol LeWitt, Roman Opalka), and Pop Art (Jasper Johns to Andy Warhol).

CRISTÓBAL BALENCIAGA (Guetaria, Spain, 1895 – Gavea, Spain, 1972). Fashion designer. At the beginning of the thirties he was already considered to be the greatest Spanish couturier. He moved to Paris in 1936–7. His training as a tailor allowed him to design, cut, assemble and sew an item of clothing himself. Advocate of a simple, balanced and contained style, he often used sober colours: from his range of browns to his use of contrast between white and the dark colours, including black. His 1939 look with sloping shoulders, sculpted waistline and pronounced hips anticipated Dior's New Look of 1947. The first to create constructive asymmetries and pointed, ogival lines ('Sack', 1956), Balenciaga is considered to be a master of purism and classicism.

JEAN MICHEL BASQUIAT (New York, 1960–1987). Painter. When Jean Michel Basquiat (remembered by Julian Schnabel in the film *Basquiat*, shown at the Venice Film Festival in 1996) arrived on the American art scene he swiftly demonstrated he was much more than just another of his generation. The talent and sudden, explosive success of this artist, born to a Tahitian father and Puerto Rican mother, should have become the symbol of the entry of Afro-American culture into the higher echelons of the American establishment. Unfortunately, his unique style, hurriedly shunted back down towards the graffiti pigeonhole, besides having given international critics and markets a run for their money, was to symbolize yet again the failure of any attempt to legitimize the existence of black culture within official cultural circles. His early death, provoked by pressure and the speculation about his creative qualities, has the inevitable effect of revealing in one man a whole destiny: difference, and discrimination. Black and white maintain an unbridgeable distance, forever in conflict with each other. Different artists are still fighting to close this gap today. Whether it is Marlene Dumas or Chris Ofili, in the microcosm of the art world the struggle for equal rights never stops.

BAYEUX LACE n. Black lace made in the French town from which it has taken its name. It became fashionable after it was introduced by the Spanish Infanta, Maria Theresa of Austria when she became the wife of Louis XIV in 1660.

SAMUEL BECKETT (Dublin, 1906–1989). Dramatist and novelist. Remembered for his dark humour and also for living out his life well away from the limelight. His little play *Not Me*, in which the main character, enveloped in deep and inscrutable darkness, is a mouth, remains unforgettable. His work portrays the pessimism of the human condition in modern times. Beckett most certainly belongs to the darker side of the twentieth century.

BERBER a. Of or relating to a race akin to the Mediterranean peoples, but with distinctive regional characteristics and traits dating back to antiquity. From ancient times they have been settled in Cyrenaica, Tripolitania and the Atlas Mountains. The 'blue men' or Tuaregs of the northern Sahara are also of Berber origin. Portrayed in literature, for instance Paul Bowles' *Under the Sheltering Sky*, their identity remains mysterious, obscure and appealing. They are characterized by tall, slender bodies and an aristocratic bearing.

JOSEPH BEUYS (Krefeld, 1921 – Düsseldorf, 1986). Artist. His use of politics to defend the environment and as a way of criticizing the behaviour and beliefs of the general public have made of him a sensitive and prophetic figure. Beuys is one of the main protagonists of the post-war avant-garde movement, and it is his vision of society as 'social sculpture' and 'anthropological art' that make this unique artist from Krefeld one of the main protagonists of the post-war avant-garde movement, dedicating his time to incessant travel between Europe and the United States and holding conferences and carrying out installations of his work and happenings on both sides of the Atlantic. A Rosicrucian by faith, he has accustomed us to seeing his art as an alchemy of symbols, words and materials. The resources and processes he uses for his work mean that the newer generations of artists have seen in him an indispensable point of reference or source of inspiration for themselves, and his use of materials from blackboards to felt, from documentary photography to design, from his use of stamps to the superimposition of words and texts onto his works have ensured Beuys' contribution to the growing contemporary awareness of ecology and natural materials. His influence is palpable not only in art but also in fashion, design and the language of the theatre.

BLACK AFRICAN CINEMA A young cinema par excellence, it came into being with the freedom and national independence movements of the 1960s (or post–1970 in the case of the Portuguese colonies). Linguistically and dynamically original, absorbing elements from the 'Nouvelle Vague' that was then in full swing in Europe – in particular its 'low cost' ideas and technology – African cinema was characterized in its first phase, the phase of mothers and fathers (Sambene Ousmane, Oumaru Ganda, Sarah Maldoror, Pauline Vieyra, Ababacar Sab, Haile Gerima, Med Hondo, Safi Faye, etc.), by its committed ideology, with traces of neorealism and a Rossellinian ethical and didactic tension. In a continent that has been left shamefully underdeveloped by the West, with high rates of illiteracy and an impressive array of languages and dialects, the film makers have assumed the role of bards whose work transcends interethnic divisions. They have become the popular voice of rediscovered independence and have warned the people about the dangers of neocolonialism. They have attacked the use of religion and 'tribal traditions' as instruments of repression, and have glorified the new-found role of women released from the shackles of an obscurantist feudalism, and pointed out, one after the other, the probable crimes of the new power-hungry, black bourgeois class – the power that has been gained by this class playing games with democracy, rather than reinterpreting it, maintained with a repressive demagogy rather than with courageous and irreversible reforms (Captain Thomas Sankara, ex-president of Burkina Faso, has however paid a high price for this latter approach). The film makers have ended up being the sole trustees (along with exiled or jailed musicians and writers – Wole Soyinka and Fela Kuti – and the immense diaspora of exiles in search of paid work) of the ethical and religious greatness of the fathers of independence on the continent, of its thinkers, often its martyrs, of Pan-Africanism and African Socialism, of anyone from Padmore to C.R.L. James, from N'Krumah to Lumumba, from Neto to Sankara. Their images have become like an Esperanto for the nations, full of immense hope and the possibility of creating a new utopia.

BLACK AND TAN n. An armed force of around 6000 men recruited by the English government to help the Irish police force put down the nationalist rebellion of 1920.

BLACK BOTTOM n. A modern dance, similiar to the foxtrot, popular in the twenties.

BLACK CULTURE Malcolm X, Martin Luther King, Rosetta King, Angela Davis, Jazz, Motown, Hip-hop ... art, poetry, cinema, literature, photography: it is everywhere. Black culture is a synthesis of all the elements of one indigenous universe, a politically active universe sensitive to its cultural origins and prepared to defend its rights and language against attempts at westernization and the supremacy of white culture (see also essay by Elisabetta Planca, p. 19).

BLACKFOOT n. The name given by white settlers to North American tribes of Indians of Algonquian stock.

BLACK HUMOUR The name given to a sense of humour distinguished by its macabre, cruel, cynical and negative style. One of the more popular examples is the TV serial *The Addams Family*, shown in America in the fifties.

BLACK LITERATURE A dialogue between two continents, from Dakar to New York, black literature consists of a uniting thread of stories, characters and traditions that spread through the universal nature of narrative. Even if half of all black fiction is born in the United States, the precious ties that bind it with the imagination and wisdom stemming from ancestral African culture cannot easily be broken (see essay by Elisabetta Planca, p. 89)

BLACK MOUNTAIN COLLEGE (North Carolina). Here, in the 1953 summer session, the very youthful Merce Cunningham (choreographer and dancer), Robert Rauschenberg (artist who went on to become founder of the New Dada movement), Paul Taylor (dancer), and John Cage and David Tudor (musicians), among others, were all gathered under one roof. It was the birth of the multimedia 'happening', an attempt to let movement, objects, sounds and words coexist in the same space-time continuum. This event, also attributed to the colour BLACK, is one of the fundamental chapters of American art history and modern culture in general. (Further reading: Calvin Tomkins *Off The Wall*, Penguin Books, New York, 1980; James Klosty, *Merce Cunningham*, Saturday Review Press, E.P. Dutton & Co. Inc., New York, 1975).

BLACK MUSIC In the eighties and nineties black music has made gradual but irreversible inroads into pop and rock music, which by tradition were white and WASP arenas. At the same time rap, reggae and soul have earned great popular credibility with their audiences. It is fashionable (the frontiers of rap have lately been spilling over into acid jazz), intellectual (look at the involvement of singer-songwriters like Ben Harper or Tracy Chapman), gets into the blood (as in ethnic African rhythms) and is danceable (e.g. Whitney Houston's mellow soul). To obtain these results, mass recognition and appreciation at an international level, has not been easy. Neither has it been painless. Only fifty years ago white America contemptuously called the blues and gospel sung by black singers or groups 'race music'. However, at the same time they were already hooked on Louis Armstrong, Count Basie and Charlie Parker's jazz. Or the jazz of Nat King Cole, The Platters, James Brown, Ray Charles and Dinah Washington. The history of black music begins here, at the end of the Second World War. And it is not surprising that the music most listened to in the fifties was made by coloured musicians (see Chuck Berry, Little Richard, Fats Domino). In the sixties the list grows longer with Motown, including the Jackson Five, Temptations, Stevie Wonder, Marvin Gaye, etc. Without mentioning that in the same decade it was a non-white guitarist, Jimi Hendrix, who taught his white fellow-musicians about technique and feeling. A lesson that is still bearing fruit, with no sign that any faith has been lost in what is one of the musical legends of this century.

BLACK PHOTOGRAPHY With its beginnings in the work of James Van Der Zee (1886–1983) and Roy De Carava (1947 onwards), black photography can be seen, in historical terms, as fairly recent. Van Der Zee's landscape is the Harlem Renaissance, a world of rituals – funerals, weddings and family gatherings – that show the autonomy of black culture alongside signs of its hybridization with white culture. De Carava introduces us to daily, working life, subway life, but also to the orbit of John Coltrane, whom he shot in various, smoky jazz club scenes. In the same years Gordon Parks was busy immortalizing the most interesting parts of Harlem. Meanwhile, on the other side of the ocean, in sub-Saharan Africa, native photography was in the process of being born. Young Senegalese and Malians frequented the studios of Mama Casset in Dakar and Seydou Keita in Bamako to get their portraits done. This has left a captivating record of the traditional dress and ornaments of the time: ornately woven plaits with coloured wool, gold ornaments and flowery calicos. Proof of the westernization of the two countries, the men wore dandy zoot suits (see text by Elisabetta Planca, p. 152).

BLACK VENUS Billie Holiday, Josephine Baker, Eartha Kitt, Donna Summer, Diana Ross, Tina Turner, Iman, Grace Jones, Whitney Houston, Angela Bassett, Janet Jackson, Veronica Webb ...

BLACK-AND-TAN COONHOUND n. A hunting-dog that tracks its prey by scent.

BLACKOUT n. The term has become synonymous with a power cut, whether planned or accidental. Given its potential for causing catastrophe, it has also become a metaphor or idiomatic phrase to describe temporary loss of memory, or partial or total disinformation.

ALIGHIERO BOETTI (Turin, 1940–1995). Unique contemporary artist, a model for future generations of artists, his work was shown in the first ever exhibition of Arte Povera in Italy in 1967, organized by Germano Celant. The label has stuck, but it has not limited his nomadic creative style, or his eclectic and experimental nature. In his biography we find a memorable anecdote, told by the artist himself, about a radical and decisive change in the direction of his work that happened around 1964–5. He had dismantled his studio because he felt he needed time to immerse himself in his artistic search. With all the technical superstructure gone, he ended up starting all over again from scratch, with just a sheet of squared paper and one mark made with a pencil. His choice of ambivalence is fundamental to his work. Alighiero & Boetti, the right hand and the left hand, concept and execution as separate processes; these hint at a dual personality. Boetti is an artist who defies all categorisation, but he is also undoubtedly a master of the experience of norms and their violation, of light and dark, of sound and silence.

ALBERTO BURRI (Città de Castello, 1915 – Nice, 1995). Modern artist. One of the great innovators of modernity, known for his work using media such as perspex and renowned for his experimentation with cracks and flaws, and with combustion. His work marks the passage from non-representational art to modern research, and he is one of the precursors of experimentation with natural or poor materials, narrative in concept, along with Fontana, Manzoni, Rauschenberg and Twombly.

CHADOR n. A large shawl worn by Muslim women to conceal their bodies when in public. Banned in the twenties in favour of a more westernized style of dress, it has returned as a compulsory article of clothing imposed by the new fundamentalist movements. In the summer months it can been seen in lighter colours and floral designs, combined with other, European-style clothing. To liberated women, however, this traditionally Islamic garment remains black in its spirit. In reality the chador is a symbol of the dependence and submissiveness of Muslim women to the male power predominant in Islam.

FRANCESCO CLEMENTE (Naples, 1952). Painter. Divides his time between New York, Madras, Rome and Amalfi. His career took off with the Italian Transavanguardia movement of the early eighties and he moved with his family to the United States in 1984. There he started making a name as one of the most highly acclaimed and stimulating artists on the international scene. His highly contemporary symbolism is richly imbued with conflicting associations such as alchemy and cabbala, Hinduism and Catholicism, eroticism and male and female sexuality. He knows how to produce mysterious hybrids which end up as metaphors of human nature, icons dedicated to the saturnine, mood-defined, lunar or nocturnal side of the artistic imagination.

CLERGYMAN n. An ecclesiastic, priest, minister, pastor. In Italian this English word has come into use as an adjective. To be 'in clergyman' means to be wearing the priestly uniform, or to have a style of dress (black outfit with white collar) that is reminiscent of a priest's cassock.

CONCEPTUAL a. In the specific case of the colour black in connection with art, Joseph Kosuth's black epistemological canvases spring to mind immediately, (where the name of a thing, its definition and accepted meanings, the object present in concrete form all serve to examine the ambiguity inherent in language itself). Also the blackboards of Joseph Beuys.

CONTRAST n. The result of the sharply different nature of colours, light, shadows.

PIERRE COULIBEUF (Normandy, 1949) and Michelangelo Pistoletto (Biella, 1932). Follow other historic collaborations between avant-garde artists and cinema directors, such as Buñuel with Picasso and Cocteau. In this case Coulibeuf, a pupil of Pierre Klossowski, directed a short film called *L'Homme Noir* with Michelangelo Pistoletto, one of the chief figures in the Arte Povera movement. Pistoletto has come a long way since his early self-portraits, also entitled *L'Homme Noir*. In this film he presents a dramatized version of himself; unencumbered by his earlier work, he returns to the images of the past and to memories. His '*homme noir*' is a disturbing presence, transforming itself into a shadow of the past that merges and interacts with the identity of the present. In this instance art assumes the characteristics of travel, of movement, of alienation. It is a place of passage. The '*homme noir*' represents the artist's alter ego, an impersonal figure undergoing continual metamorphoses. Unlike the Black Man of classical narrative (*q.v.* Negative-Positive), Pistoletto's version shows us the fascinating and productive bond that exists between the artist and his invisible double. Invisible, but somehow not disturbing in its invisibility.

ENZO CUCCHI (Morro d'Alba, 1953). Artist. Lives and works in Ancona and Rome. Along with Sandro Chia, Francesco Clemente and Mimmo Paladino, he is one of the most important and prominent artists of the neoexpressionist movement of the eighties, the Transavanguardia, which became known through art critic Achile Bonito Oliva. Cucchi's work is often anthropomorphic in subject matter. It consists of studies of the contrasts between nature and culture based on poetically apocalyptic hypotheses.

ANGELA DAVIS (USA, 1944). A teacher who became the symbol, in the late sixties and the early seventies, of student protests. Her public interventions in defence of democracy and her powerful and passionate defence of the rights of the Afro-American community are unforgettable. Like Jimi Hendrix, Angela Davis has become a legendary icon of her times. She influenced generally accepted taste at the time, and her halo of frizzy hair and her simple wardrobe, a mixture of western dress and ethnic patterns, has become the uniform of female protest, whether political or in defence of feminism.

DECADENT a. Said of what is in a state of decadence. A derivative of decadentism, it concerns all the most luxurious or sumptuous aspects of the colour black.

DESIGN From the beginning of this century the colour black has played a key role in cutting-edge design, as can be seen in the work of the Bauhaus, Eileen Gray, Charles Rennie Mackintosh, Charles Eames, Giò Ponti, Marco Zanuso, Archizoom, Gaetano Pesce, Ron Arad, Tom Dixon, Nigel Coates, Rolf Sachs and others. The objects that have been the most successful in breaking new ground in technical design – mostly chairs, armchairs, tables, lamps and the like – have all favoured the use of black and white as neutral colours that best emphasize a design's quality and identity. Designers like Eileen Gray or Andrée Putman have realized their 'total' vision of a habitat in a range of whites, greys, blacks and ecrus. In British design of the eighties, black and rough-cast iron objects appeared, linked to neogothic notions of recycling and urban decadence. Architects like Pesce or Gehry have used black to emphasize the use and physical presence in the environment of plastics and flexible woods, which are characterized by lightness or transparency. Functionalism and technological design of the sixties and seventies also used black as a stylistic passe-partout. This custom lives on today – from television sets to PCs, from electronic agendas to telephones, design still wraps itself in black ...

CHRISTIAN DIOR (Granville, Normandy, 1905 – Paris, 1957). Fashion designer. After training with Piguet and Lelong and collaborating with Balmain, he was given the chance to set up his own atelier by cotton magnate Marcel Boussac. His first collection came out in 1947. First called 'the flared line', it became known as the 'New Look'. Skirts flared out from tight waistbands and rigid bodices supported by stays; hems dropped and pleats, drapes and panels were in, often worn over tulle petticoats. The 1948 collection was called 'Envol': skirts were gathered at the back and worn with loose-cut, high-collared jackets. He alternated his innovations from year to year. Hems went up, and the famous Chinese-style pillbox hat and the equally famous 'Princess' line – a modern version of the Empire style dress, gathered under the bosom – came in. In 1954 Dior was the leader of the revival in fashion for men. His varying inspirations decreed the 'H line', the 'A Line' the 'Y line'– all of which have now entered the history books. In his designs he favoured the use of black, white and navy. He finished off his collections with accessories like brooches that were fixed to collars, shoulders or waists. Pearls became a *sine qua non* in the wardrobe of the fashionable female after he brought them in in the fifties. For years his ideas have influenced the different seasons. Today the artistic direction of the House of Dior is in the hands of John Galliano.

DOLCE & GABBANA (Domenico Dolce, Polizzi Generosa, Palermo, 1958; Stefano Gabbana, Milan, 1963). Their line in fashion is designed for 'real' women – women who are expressive and sensual. Their clothes are sexy and austere at the same time. The colours and shapes they use are derived from a Mediterranean tradition. Corsets, bustier dresses, lace, silk and crocheted wool, all gain additional narrative strength through the use of classic Sicilian black.

MARLENE DUMAS (Capetown, 1953). Artist. Considered to be one of the most sensitive and interesting artists on the international scene. Her work consists of portraits on paper, characterized by an outstanding and idiosyncratic use of watercolour. She depicts friends, celebrities and, more recently, fashion and advertising beauties. In her work she often modifies the features and skin colour of famous faces in white culture in such a way that they become the gods and goddesses of black culture. Dumas brings to our attention the fact that this same process has been going on for centuries to the detriment of black culture, black language and ways of expression, black behavioural patterns, black music, ideology and philosophy of life. A portrait by Dumas will reveal all of this, and more: the denial of their origin by blacks who are trying to be white (*q.v.* Michael Jackson), or the attempt to conform and comply with the demands and expectations of a white, Western audience (*q.v.* Josephine Baker). But Dumas goes even further than that in her ability to penetrate the pain and pride of a whole race through the mere expression of a face or the intensity of a gaze. Like African ritual masks, the subject matter of Dumas' imagination goes beyond the boundaries of white mythology into a world where meaning is found and expressed on many levels. She has an almost magical ability to galvanize our attention and win our respect. On the colour black, Dumas has written: 'Black is not a color – the painting teachers said. / No Blacks allowed – the signs used to read. / Matisse made a show (1946) titled – Black is a colour. / Tiger Woods is not black enough, some black guys said. / Why can't he be, just black, the others said. [...] / Color is a very sensitive matter. / Let's have more color I said / but as David Hammons work showed / The white art world, still dresses / in their funeral fashions.' (see p. 88)

EMANCIPATION n. Liberation from a position of inferiority, whether legal or social, from submission or from material or moral constraints towards the progressive attainment of equality.

EMPHASIS – EMPHATIC n. The adjective 'emphatic' and the term 'emphasis' are more contemporary than their old synonyms of 'rigour' or 'conceptual' when used to describe the colour black. Something that is emphatic is profoundly informative, possessing great narrative power that can accentuate a multiplicity of values and meanings. This is why minimalist artists stopped using black, as their aim was to reduce the physical presence of their work to an absolute zero. Of all the colours in nature, black seems to have the most inexhaustibly rich range of meaning. It is impetuous, full of passion, sometimes overwhelming, a warm colour, excellent for lending clarity and for conveying frequently antithetical feelings and ideals. If this were not the case, it would have been less frequently used in art and fashion, or photography and design. It would have suffered a more uncertain fate, and been subject to all the vagaries of taste and fashion. As it stands, black represents the classical spirit, but also change and renewal; it represents the norm, but also its rupture; the absence of colour or its complete domination; tradition and evolution, etc.

EROTICISM n. The exaltation of sexual tendencies and impulses. In art and literature, an insistence on sexually arousing or suggestive symbolism.

ETHNIC GROUP – ETHNIC 1. n. 2. a. In any culture, from Muslim to Japanese, there are countless important manifestations of the colour black. One example is the ritualistic and celebratory black of the Japanese kimono.

EXISTENTIALISM n. A movement in contemporary philosophy which developed in France after the Second World War (Sartre, Merleau-Ponty, De Beauvoir and Wahl). In opposition to idealism and realism, it insists upon the specific value of individual human existence and stresses the precarious nature of this existence. In terms of costume it marks the apotheosis of black as a symbol of the unease and suffering of modern life.

EXPERIMENTAL a. Used to describe activities aimed at trying out new systems in a determined field.

FASHION n. A prevailing custom or style of dress, etiquette, procedure, etc. Conventional usage in dress, manners, etc. (extract from Webster's Encyclopedic Unabridged Dictionary of the English Language, Gramercy Books, New York, 1994, p. 517). There is no item of clothing or accessory in the technical or stylistic repertory of fashion for which a black version or range has not been planned. Nevertheless, what needs to be examined and then emphasized in this context is the role played by the colour black in the twentieth century as the guiding principle of radical changes in tastes and style. The transitional stages can be best expressed by a list of images, each expressing a period: a. Edwardian elegance at Ascot (in the first season after Edward VII's death). b. Chanel's little black dress. c. Bows on Coco Chanel's hats. d. Marlene Dietrich's dinner jacket. e. Garbo's impenetrably dark glasses. f. Marlon Brando's and James Dean's studs. g. Dramatic chic couture from Balenciaga. h. Hispanizing jet embroidery and jewellery from Balenciaga. i. Existentialist and beatnik roll-neck sweaters. j. Givenchy tube-dress on Audrey Hepburn. k. Catsuits and skin-tight dresses in matt colouring. l. Yves Saint Laurent's nude look. m. Punk nail varnish, hairstyles and make-up. n. Gothic. o. Doc Martens. p. Morticia look. q. Pervy vinyl. r. Comme des Garçons; Yohji Yamamoto. s. Minimalism. t. Nylon passe-partout: hooded coat by Prada. u. Sicilian sexy style by Dolce & Gabbana. v. Jean-Paul Gaultier and Thierry Mugler's S/M (see text by Lela Acquarone, pp. 122–4). A quick glance at these points of reference immediately shows the radicality, the multiethnicity, sensuality, rigour, personality and distinction all accorded to this one colour. As has been demonstrated in the art, design, dance, theatre, photography and photomontages of leading creators, black is a sign of transformation, conquest, provocation and also of the way fashion identity exists as a series of necessary tabulae rasae which are repeated as part of a cycle. Common usage and custom in society derives a great part of its energy from fashion, but most of all it unquestionably marks out periods of unease as well as optimism, or extravagance compared to moderation. It indicates the profundity or the superficiality of taste, nostalgia for the past and a foretaste of the future, or femininity and sexual ambiguity.

FEMININE – FEMININITY 1. a. 2. n. A list of elements traditionally referring to femininity and linked to the colour black.

FILM NOIR A genre of cinematography born in France in 1946. Characterized by unclear situations with psychological undertones that convey a feeling of apprehension, and usually degenerate into homicidal or criminal acts (see essay, p. 110).

FISCHLI & WEISS (Peter Fischli, Zurich, 1952 / David Weiss, Zurich, 1946). Artists using a wide variety of media, from black rubber to polystyrene, from photography to film and pictures or photos of the environment. Their versatility is an authentic expression of contemporary art. Their poetic inspiration leads them to create situations which are either completely ambiguous or paradoxical, existing in a precarious equilibrium. They tend to be scenic reconstructions of the 'real thing'.

LUCIO FONTANA (Rosario di Santa Fé, 1899 – Comabbio, Varese, 1968). Sculptor and painter. In the thirties he established contact with the Lombard abstractionists (his first exhibition was at Il Milione gallery) and with the international Abstraction-Création movement. Here we see the passage from representation to pure invention, to a language of colour, symbol and material, where the physicality of these elements is of overriding importance. From using cement, Fontana goes on to investigate the use of ceramics (Albisola, 1935–6, and Sèvres). In Argentina, during the war, he made his neofuturist declaration, with its emphasis on 'unity of time and space', in favour of art appropriate to the times. After that he produced his 'spatialist' work and installations, meant to be neither paintings nor sculptures but 'shapes, colours and sounds across space' (Technical Manifesto of Spatialism, 1951. The first installation was created in the Milanese gallery, Naviglio in 1949). From Fontana's Concetti Spaziali are born the perforations and slashings of canvases and other two-dimensional media, intended to create a breach transporting the viewer beyond the virtual surface.

GILBERT & GEORGE (q.v. Gothic – Late Gothic – Gothic Revival)

GOTHIC – NEO-GOTHIC – GOTHIC REVIVAL Three different stylistic periods linked by a common thread that goes from the original Gothic to mannerisms related to Gothic inspiration. The ogival arches and ceilings, endless heights, spires and pinnacles – decorated with plant motifs and fantastic animals – of classic Gothic architecture find their inspiration in Nordic symbols or the natural landscape. Brought back in the Gothic Revival by interpreters like Antonio Gaudí (Sagrada Familia, Parco Güell), they then invaded, under different definitions, modern (Charles Rennie Mackintosh to Carlo Mollino) and contemporary costume and habitat (the flamboyant style of Garoust and Bonetti; the first decorative iron objects created by Tom Dixon; Nigel Coates' essays on urban design as a digression and stratification of architectural styles, objects of daily use, historical documents and human physiognomies). 'Gothic' and 'Late Gothic' are definitions also used in poetry and literature. Artaud's beloved Late Gothic can be seen as either the precursor of the popular novel (later to become TV melodrama or soaps), or as the inspiration for film noir and pulp fiction ('B' movies raised to cult status). In contemporary fashion, the word Gothic immediately brings to mind an evolution of the dark style. Black clothing, black interiors, crucifixes, serpents, heavily made-up eyes, not to mention a film-script that pays homage to Dreyer or cult movies like Doctor Caligari's Surgery. In art it is Gilbert & George who incarnate a passion for Gothic stained-glass windows which clearly inspire both the structure and colouring of their work.

MARTHA GRAHAM (Pittsburgh, 1894 – New York, 1900). Dancer, choreographer and stage director. The creator of a new technique in the dance movement based on contraction and decontraction. Her collaborations with Isamu Noguchi, artist, scenographer and creator of unforgettable sets, mark the beginning of a formal connection between modern dance and imported, Japanese reduction of gesture and minimalist conception of space. A fashionable figure, as well as being a sublime dancer, Graham chose black as the dominant colour in her wardrobe both on stage and in real life. Her impeccably gathered hair, light make-up and kohl-lined eyes add to the magical presence she has acquired over time. She is a western geisha, devoted to self-realization, and a much sought-after presence in intellectual and showbusiness circles. With Diana Vreeland she is certainly one of the longest-lived and most inspired women in recent American history.

KEITH HARING (Pittsburgh, 1963 – New York, 1987). Artist. The only white representative of the Graffiti culture that emerged from the New York metropolis in the seventies and eighties. A follower of Dubuffet, he enjoyed sketching and painting on immensely long rolls of paper. Subway walls and building fronts were an almost natural extension of this. With great manual dexterity, Haring developed a politically and ecologically orientated pictorial world. He often used sexual metaphors to express the active relationships of power and the passive relationships of those who submit to it. His tag (a kind of recognition icon or signature) is a 'radiant child' (radioactive child).

HELL'S ANGELS A real all-American movement. Hell's Angels are regulated by a sometimes violent code of ethics and regenerated by a continual stream of new adepts. They are a potent icon of American fashion. With their Harley Davidsons, leather outfits, tattoos, carefully cultivated moustaches and beards, muscular bodies and threatening scowls, the Angels keep themselves to themselves and spend their time travelling the United States using their 'insider' maps and special stop-over points.

ALFRED HITCHCOCK (UK, 1899–1980). Film director. 'I don't make mystery films. In those the audience wonders what will happen next. If I were to make a movie about Cinderella the audience knows it will get at least one cadaver in the golden carriage.' With a classic sense of humour (confirmed by his traditional appearances in fleeting and totally diverse roles in his films), Hitchcock trained his public well. They knew to expect the frisson of anxiety, the unexpected, the shivers and all-out fear. 'My only aim,' he said, 'is to make people curious and distressed ... I never have a moral purpose.' Although he is linked to the American film noir movement, Hitchcock stands apart with his psychoanalytical ability, his taste for metaphor and his ability to more or less consciously induce nightmares and neurotic impulses. Among his most famous films are Notorious, I Will Save You, Psycho, Marnie, and Window over the Courtyard.

JENNY HOLZER (USA, 1948). Artist. 'Protect me from what I want', 'Men don't protect you anymore', 'The future is stupid': these and other slogans speaking out against the equivocal and subliminal message of American culture appear on illuminated billboards, chiselled in marble, or on metal plaques. Like a virus, the messages infest all types of consumer goods: baseball hats, pencils, t-shirts, condoms. Holzer calls her messages 'Truisms'.

REBECCA HORN (Hamburg, 1944). Multimedia artist. Author of mechanical sculptures but also films, of which the best known are: Die Paradies-Witwe and Der Eintanzer, made between 1974 and 1979. Horn's objects, appearing in her films or made specifically for them, have a powerful and stark poetic impact (see the essay on art by Mariuccia Casadio, p. 58–61)

IDEAL a. From idea, that which exists only in thought or the imagination; the fruit of fantasy, imaginary. n. 1. That which is configured in the mind as a model of perfection; what could be, often opposed to what is; what is most adapted to a given situation. 2. noble sentiment or intention.

IDEOGRAM n. Graphic symbol representing an idea, not a phonetic value.

JAPONAISERIE n. From the French word describing Japanese or imitation-Japanese objects, including black lacquer, a fascination with opacity in fabrics, facial make-up and rice paper. Japan has a wealth of shadowy, translucent, mysterious imagery to draw on which continues to capture the Western imagination today.

JAZZ (q.v. Black music)

JET, BLACK AMBER. A type of coal endowed with a remarkable shine, thus often used this century in the manufacture of jewellery.

DONNA KARAN (Forest Hills, NY, 1948). Fashion designer. Trained at the Parsons School of Design. In her second year she had already been hired as a sketch artist by Anne Klein's atelier. In 1984 she started her own business, carving herself a niche in the New York fashion scene with her minimalist style and predilection for monochrome clothing, essentially black, navy, white and ecru.

REI KAWAKUBO (Tokyo, 1942). Fashion designer. She studied literature and advertising at Keio University, graduating in 1964. In 1969, after some years working freelance, she founded Comme des Garçons. Determined to redefine traditional female wear, she brought in a conceptual style characterized by asymmetrical groupings, layering, torsions, trains, and expansions and contractions of form. She works her fabric or other materials like an artist, breaking the conventional delineation of space. Her choices are always visceral and emotive, but also profoundly intelligent. Her way of making changes and taking risks is unique in the context of contemporary fashion. With her immense, innovative flair Kawakubo has also made designer objects, like chairs and other furniture, which are used in her Tokyo, New York and Paris boutiques.

ANSELM KIEFER (Donaueschingen, Germany, 1945). Artist. First active in the seventies, he became very popular in the eighties as an outstanding representative of the return to neoexpressionist tastes and painting. Eclectic, a narrative artist, delighting in a vast range of materials (from paper to straw, planks of wood to unstretched canvas, from photography to the environment), Kiefer also loves caligraphy, collages, and layering images and techniques. Along with Beuys, Richter, Hans and Hilla Becker and a few others, he is considered to be a founder of the new German generation. He shares with these artists a taste for obscurity, shadows, decadence and, at the same time, a scrupulous control over the development of his work.

KIMONO n. A traditional, long Japanese robe with wide sleeves and a sash around the waist (*obi*). 'The female puppets consist only of a head and a pair of hands. The body, legs, and feet are concealed within a long kimono, and so the operators need only work their hands within the costume to suggest movements. To me this is the very epitome of reality, for a woman of the past did indeed exist only from the collar up and the sleeves out; the rest of her remained hidden in darkness. A woman of the middle or upper ranks of society seldom left her house, and when she did she shielded herself from the gaze of the public in the dark recesses of her palanquin. Most of her life was spent in the twilight of a single house, her body shrouded day and night in gloom, her face the only sign of her existence. Though the men dressed somewhat more colorfully than they do today, the women dressed more somberly. Daughters and wives of the merchant class wore astonishingly severe dress. Their clothing was in effect no more than a part of the darkness, the transition between darkness and face.' (from Junichiro Tanizaki, *In Praise of Shadows*, Leete's Island Books, 1977, p. 28).

MARTIN LUTHER KING (USA, 1929–1968). Baptist minister. He started a huge non-violent black people's civil rights movement. Awarded the Nobel Peace Prize in 1964, he was assassinated in Memphis in 1968.

CALVIN KLEIN (New York, 1942). Fashion designer. Graduated from the Fashion Institute of Technology in 1962, and began his work in 1968. An able tailor, he had a natural preference for sober and simple lines, and over time his penchant for a sophisticated minimalism increased. From the outset he adopted the use of natural colours, navy blue or black. His understated style, somewhat precious but aesthetically pure, has made him one of the most immediately recognizable of American fashion designers working today.

KOHL n. Antimony sulphide in powder form, often used as eye make-up. It has decorative and disinfectant qualities.

ANNIS KOUNELLIS (Piraeus, Athens, 1936). Artist. One of the most significant and original representatives of Italian Arte Povera, Kounellis uses organic materials (from earth and fire, to live horses, parrots, plants, coal and wood), hessian bags, plaster casts, metaphors of folk memory, music and words to transform his work continuously. It is a way of avoiding falling into the art pigeonholing system. A representational alchemist, Kounellis has chosen memory as the constant preoccupation of his work which is characterized by a great freedom of philosophical intention and physical dimensions. Some of the recurrent themes in his work are: the primaeval versus the future, the search for a harmonious blending of disparate elements, the quest for passion, the presentation of insurmountable obstacles, and the feeling of belonging to art as opposed to the laws of the outside world. Like the oracle of Ancient Greece he formulates his premonitions and intuitions through different instruments ranging from the written word through to instruments of sound. He is possibly one of the most lunar and nocturnal among contemporary artists. He was born, as it was believed in antiquity, under the influence of Saturn.

BARBARA KRUGER (USA, 1953). Artist. In the eighties she was among a number of female artists whose work bore a political message. Her black-and-white images, photographs and photocopies are covered in provocative declarations against the chauvinistic western system of values. She opened up a generation to artwork dominated by a majority of unknown female artists. She is contentious, intellectual, commanding and yells out her convictions through her work. The committed nature of the concepts she expresses give depth and semantic intensity to her art.

LACQUER n. A coloured substance of vegetable, animal or synthetic origin, used as a protective and ornamental layer on various objects. A colour made by the mechanical or chemical fixation of an organic colorant on a normally inorganic support used in painting and in printing on textiles. 'The rooms at the Waranjiya are about nine feet square, the size of a comfortable little tearoom, and the alcove pillars and ceilings glow with a faint smoky luster, dark even in the light of the lamp. But in the still dimmer light of the candlestand, as I gazed at the trays and bowls standing in the shadows cast by that flickering point of flame, I discovered in the gloss of this lacquerware a depth and richness like that of a still, dark pond, a beatuy I had not before seen. It had not been mere chance, I realized, that our ancestors, having discovered lacquer, had conceived such a fondness for objects finished in it.' (from Junichiro Tanizaki, *In Praise of Shadows*, Leete's Island Books, 1977, p. 13).

KARL LAGERFELD (Hamburg, 1938). Fashion designer and photographer. A convinced follower of eclecticism, Lagerfeld has a particular passion for the colours black and white. His visual and creative richness allows him to interpret this passion in continually different ways, with a particular penchant for twenties and thirties styles. He designs collections for Chanel and Fendi.

HELMUT LANG (Austria, date of birth unknown). Fashion designer, moved to Paris and then to New York. Urban, cultivator of cultural nomadism, pioneer of minimalism in fashion, experimenter in synthetics, his flagship is unisex basics.

LIGHT n. 1. Play of —, contrast of light and dark; 2. Any kind of light source. A symbol of the clarifying force of the spirit. (opp. darkness).

PETER LINDBERGH (Berlin, 1944). Photographer. The intensity, sensuality and strength of female beauty veritably explodes out of his black and white, sometimes documentary, sometimes metaphysical, fashion images. Considered to be one of the greatest contemporary photographers, Lindbergh works for American, French and Italian *Vogue*.

LINGERIE n. Underwear for men and for women, in the latter case usually consisting of fine materials decorated with lace.

MAN RAY (Philadelphia, 1890 – Paris, 1976). Photographer and artist, he emerged in 1913 at the Armory Show exhibition with the backing of Stieglitz. This brought him into contact with the avant-garde of the contemporary art world. Cubist, dadaist, surrealist, Man Ray is a unique case in modern art. Parallel to his paintings, assemblages and ready-made objects, his photography was marked by the discovery of rayogrammes (1921). This technique simply uses light to print images directly on the negative without having recourse to a camera, thus obtaining abstract photos in B/W. His collaboration with Brodovitch (art director of *Harper's Bazaar*) and Liberman (*Vogue*) resulted in equally interesting work. For them he produced amazing fashion numbers and cover pages in which the wording, the cut of the image and the subject matter all had an equal impact.

NELSON MANDELA (Umtata, South Africa, 1918). After years of political persecution by the upholders of apartheid, and more than 25 years behind bars, Nelson Mandela is today President of South Africa. A leading figure of black culture in our time, he has given us an exemplary, if not unique, lesson in life. He is a living myth in the history of black peoples, now redeemed and on the way towards the legitimate affirmation of their thoughts, ideas and ideological positions after years of violent repression and censorship.

ROBERT MAPPLETHORPE (1946–1989). Photographer. He started his career in the seventies, taking portraits of his friend and roommate Patti Smith. A member of the New York New Wave youth movement, Mapplethorpe gained further notoriety photographing friends and representatives of culture and the art world. It was not long before his own photography crossed over into the domain of art, with cycles like the images taken of bodybuilder Lysa Lyon, disturbing still-lifes of flowers bearing a close resemblance to sexual organs, and the S/M series of nude male figures, either self portraits or black models of a rare beauty and sensuality. His surfaces are monochrome and luminous, preferably black (Mapplethorpe wore black all his life, and black became a leading element in his house and in his collection of porcelain from the twenties and thirties), – pure geometric compositions composed of different yet interrelatable modules. The X and the cross, along with different kinds of polygons, are the unmistakable hallmark of his work.

STEVEN MEISEL (New York, 1954). Fashion photographer and a well-known figure in the fashion world, Meisel has created powerful interpretations of the fashion of our times. Behind his images we can see considerable cultural awareness and, from his contributions to historic pages in *Vogue* (Vreeland with Penn, Avedon, Bailey) he crosses the boundary into art. His use of B/W and colour are developed and expanded using a variety of styles and techniques. His use of quotations (consistent without being repetitive) is parallel to certain thematic and conceptual tendencies in US contemporary art.

METAPHORIC a. Of or containing one or more metaphors; figurative. It is expressed by means of a likeness or drawing a parallel with another thing to that named, taking the concept that it expresses beyond its true meaning. From the Greek *metaphorà*, mutation, derivative of *methaphérein*, to transfer beyond, elsewhere.

ELEANORE MIKUS (USA, 1927). American artist. 'Each time I finished a painting,' remembers Mikus, talking about her 1960–8 period, 'I recorded it in a black note book, I sketched it, I numbered it and I also wrote down any pertinent information. In those days photography was not up to capturing all the nuances within a painting.' Taking into account that Mikus is solely interested in the monochromatic use of black and white (to the point of bearing many resemblances with the work of Louise Nevelson, see glossary entry), it is easy to deduce that the two opposite colours are used like any other colour. In fact, as Mikus has revealed, it is even more difficult than with other colours to identify the complete range of tones possible. This becomes apparent when we consider the wide range of media she uses. Naturally, with each medium there are greater or lesser effects of light and shade, of density or lightness in chromatic intensity. This can be seen in the series of works called *Shadows of the Real* in which the artists uses a range of media and techniques from paving stones to masonite, to plaster to cover the canvas, to working both on the front and on the back of the canvas 'to be sure that it was completely taut and to fill the empty spaces with supporting materials'. This is a bare minimum of information for the reader who may still be convinced that the use of monochrome and abstraction in art is a less expressive and efficient technique requiring less commitment than polychrome and figurative art. For further information q.v. Nevelson, Burri, Conceptual, Minimalist, Nouveau Réalisme, Rigour, Reinhardt.

MINIMAL a. Minimum; least possible.

YUKIO MISHIMA (Tokyo 1925–1970). Author. 'Honey-coloured skin, black hair, black eyes: it must have been a boy from Asia Minor, from the country of birth of that famous Asian slave Antiochus. The ideal of youth and beauty that the Romans dreamt of in the second century was Asian,' writes Mishima in his *The Theory of Shunsuke*

Hinoki Written by Himself, translated from the collection *Forbidden Colours* (1951–2). This is one of the endless images which, more or less explicitly, make him one of the most obsessed spokesmen on beauty, redolent of the Crepuscolare poets with their all-pervading mood of disenchantment. An antihero of traditional Japanese civilization, Yukio Mishima was moved by the myths of strength and beauty as violence and death. After developing a subtle and cruel cult of eroticism, he is noted for taking his own life using the traditional ritual of *seppuku* (harakiri). He was a strong nationalist and made his decision in defiance of the westernization of the Orient and the decision taken by Japan to demilitarize.

MODERN a. Referring or belonging to the present, or to times near to our own (opp. ancient). The term has been used in many aesthetic movements as well as being a philosophic conviction encapsulated in many forms of creative expression. The modern dream (now considered by many to be bankrupt of ideas) is the encounter of functionality with aesthetic values, of the prototype object with the serialization process of industry, the triumph of technologically advanced materials in their application to the structure of new objects. In conventional terms we understand modern to mean what is synthetic, essential, but planned and calculated in all its diverse possibilities of execution. Naturally, black and white, as base colours, have a role to play in the objects, environment and fashions of modernity. They favour the elimination of any ambiguity in the design and execution of new shapes, facilitating experimentation with plastics and other synthetic derivatives. Modern is a definition connected to every projection of our surroundings or the clothes we wear into the future.

MODERN DANCE With representatives like Martha Graham, Merce Cunningham, Pina Bausch and Carole Armitage, the term 'modern dance' implies breaking the rules of the old classical syntax. It is the fruit of ethnic cross-breeding, of spectacular and eclectic concepts, and of the language of gestural art often reduced to repetition and to movements restricted within idealized geometric figures. It is also athletic performance taken to the limits of pure physicality.

MODERN DRAMA From its original interaction with space and time, modern drama has been influenced by breakthroughs in art. Today it is generally understood to involve crises of word and text and the liberation of drama from the confines of the stage so that it can cross over into various situations of daily life. This is accompanied by a more abstract vision of costume, often reduced to complete nudity. The normal sequence of time may be dismantled and temporal sequences are broken in favour of simultaneous effects involving language, gesture and sound. Fundamental contributions to modern drama have been made by Peter Brook (mythological reinterpretations); Robert Wilson (interaction of music, dance and objects of art in a space and a rigid avoidance of potential time in favour of a simple flow of gestures and movements across real time); Peter Stein (theatre and politics are one and the same for this most intellectual and rigorous follower of Brecht), and above all Pina Bausch (made contributions to contemporary theatrical costume and to fashion: men dressed as women, women as men, outer and inner garments worn creased and crumpled, zips broken. Black is the predominant colour – as a criticism of bourgeois taste, as a statement of proletarian rage; ball gowns that hide or obliterate the conventional pose or charm of the human figure – these examples can only give us a vague idea of the sheer genius behind her innovative force). Modern drama can thus be defined as the presence of action, dance, performance, sounds and noises, chance happenings, silences, video and film images, tightrope acts from classical circus and acrobatics from twentieth-century dance, all interacting with each other at the same time. In this sense figures like Merce Cunningham, Trisha Brown, Lucinda Childs, Carole Armitage, Rebecca Horn, Gilbert & George, Michelangelo Pistoletto (*Zoo*), and others can be regarded as figures exerting more or less influence on the way drama is presented today. From modern American dance to the way the artist interacts with daily life to the use of the body in art, there are many ways in which one can come to understand the full range of the vocabulary used in contemporary theatre. (See also text by Walter le Moli, p. 115).

UGO MULAS (Milan, 1928–1973). Photographer. First active in the mid-fifties. He is remarkable for his hyperactivity and vast sphere of interests: portraiture, fashion, art, theatre, cinema, literature, poetry. His B/W photography is considered to be amongst the most refined and radical of the second half of the twentieth century. Mulas left a vast collection of negatives and vintage prints, extremely expensive to conserve. His family (wife Antonia and daughter Melina, both photographers) have established a foundation that merits more state donations and intervention. Aesthetically sensitive, but also a theoretician of the image, Ugo Mulas has left a fascinating series of essays. This is a small example of his declaration of intent: 'The idea of this half-black, half-white sheet of paper was in my head for a long time; until I decided to do something analogous, only in a superficial way, to try and obtain an image that would be the synthesis of what the darkroom represents. A darkroom is the place where one generally concludes what has already been started out-of-doors with cameras and films; a darkroom is rarely used by itself to work directly on paper or film with just light, developers and fixing agents alone, without relying upon films that have already been exposed through cameras and without relying on lenses.' (Translated from G. Celant, *Ugo Mulas*, Federico Motta Editore, Milano, 1989, p. 158).

NEGATIVE-POSITIVE The colour black has an ambiguous and ambivalent nature, synonymous with bipolarity, giving it a mythological aura that has, over the centuries, fed aesthetics, ideologies, politics, techno, technology, theatre, cinema, etc. Negative examples are: black shirts, black widows, black magic, the black plague, black mass, Black Friday, black bread, black jet, black cat, black period, dark lady, black man, black list, etc. Positive examples are: little black dress, black Venus, black gold, Africa sickness, Black Pride, black humour, Black Jack, Black Virgin, black pearl, Black is Black, etc.

NEOREALISM / NOUVEAU REALISME The first term refers to an important chapter in the history of cinema, the second to a modern art movement. Although the two movements come about in slightly different periods (De Sica, Zavatti, Rossellini and other Italian cinematographers make their mark in the forties, whereas the French art movement takes place in the fifties and sixties with artists like Arman, Tinguely, Yves Klein and Rotella), they have certain philosophical affinities. From the black-and-white documentary style of cinema we move over to diverse impressions of reality in the artistic world. This covers anything from '*repêchage*' of similar objects assembled together or the creation of machines in single units, to immaterial and spiritual visions contrasted with concrete and impersonal reality. Both movements, however, provide us with images that seem to be hinged philosophically on an existential poetry of loss, mutation, waste and misery. The alchemy of reels of film and the alchemy of pure pigments, along with crises and vindications of identity, create a cultural setting that places Europe in the forefront of worldwide artistic experimentation for this period.

LOUISE NEVELSON (USA, 1900–1988). Sculptor. She created three-dimensional compositions made out of assembled scrap wood and moulds. Nevelson's monochrome work (sometimes white, but mostly black) had a strong influence on the Pop generation. Her physical presence was as unforgettable as her work: a long, lean figure, she wore a scarf knotted around her neck; her wardrobe was predominantly black, accessorized with silver and turquoise jewellery, and her eyes permanently enhanced by a double-layer of false eyelashes and countless layers of mascara.

NEW WAVE (or 'No Wave' in its more radical manifestations). A fashion in music and dress born in the United States at the end of the seventies. Inspired by the punk movement, New Wave sees the appearance of nihilistic and obscure rock groups. Discordant sounds, improvisations, and provocative denunciations of the recording industry link this trend to the modern musical inclinations of John Cage, Philip Glass, Monte Young and others. Parallel to this they use TV jingles, advertising breaks and serial theme tunes to create a caustic and dryly intellectual sound. The New Wave is also important as a contemporary philosophy of creation with its eclectic and dilettante leanings. Its multidisciplinary and interactive culture includes, among others, film directors (Jim Jarmusch), photographers (Jimi de Sana, Robert Mapplethorpe), musicians (Brian Eno, Talking Heads, Père Ubu, DNA, John Zorn, Sakamoto), artists (Jean Michel Basquiat, Keith Haring, Barbara Ess) and poets (René Ricard, Lydia Lunch).

HELMUT NEWTON (Berlin, 1920). Became a photographer after an adventurous and nomadic apprenticeship via the Heinrich von Treitschke Realgymnasium (1928–32), the American School (1933–35), the studio of Berlin photographer Eva, and the war, during which he moved to Australia. In Sydney he started working professionally and, after several short visits to Paris to work with magazines like *Elle, Marie Claire, Jardin de Mode* and *Vogue*, he finally decided to settle in the 'City of Lights' to work full time for *Stern* and French and American *Vogue*. With his taste for drama and voyeurism, which touches on an aesthetically shocking conceptual sado-masochism, Newton is the interpreter par excellence of female eroticism: black leather and fishnet stockings, extremely long varnished nails, attitudes of dominance, ambiguity, androgyny, homosexuality and soft-core pornography. With the return of glamour and the sexy look, Newton's work is in demand more than ever and is a point of reference for younger generations.

NOCTURNAL a. Pertaining to the night. The term is employed figuratively to describe a crepuscular and decadent humour or feeling in human beings. In art it is habitually used to describe a certain genre of naturalistic representations, or the nocturnal qualities themselves of a work: dark, disquieting and inscrutable.

NON-CONFORMIST n. (*q.v.* Anti, Black Culture, Hell's Angels, Punk, Rock, Pulp, Antonioni, Artaud, Art, Basquiat, Beckett, Beuys, Boetti, A. Davis, M. Dumas, Hitchcock, Kawakubo, etc.).

OBVIOUS a. 1. said of surfaces that completely absorb the light, therefore do not reflect it and appear to be totally without colour. 2. What is of the darkest colour in existence: — as ink; — clouds; — collar, dirty; shades, glasses with dark lenses; — sheep, said of one who is different to those around him because of negative qualities and is looked upon unfavourably by others; *bête noire*, person or persons feared or detested; — book, the book in which the names of people considered to be dangerous or enemies are recorded; — well (opp. white). 3. Mournful, painful, sad, melancholic; bad, wicked: a black disposition; to be in a mood; a black soul; black ingratitude; to see the dark side of everything; crime columns; accident and crime-oriented dark news columns; market, clandestine and illicit; the market, in wartime, clandestine trading at very high prices of rationed goods.
n. 1. The colour black; any substance of that colour: — sepia / not to be able to distinguish black from white, not to have critical faculties; (opp. white). 2. In chess and draughts, the player who has the black pieces and is the adversary of the whites. 3. In accounting, figures that are hidden from the official accounts, illegal. From Old English.

GEORGIA O'KEEFE (Sun Prairie, Wisconsin, 1887 – Santa Fé, New Mexico (1986). Visual artist. Close to the New York avant-garde of the 1910s, which was focused around

Stieglitz's gallery (she later married him), in the following decades she developed her initial lyrical abstractionism derived from her obsession with natural shapes and elemental architectural structures. These characteristics are also found in her subsequent work, which turned her into one of America's most celebrated artists. Her favourite themes were natural forms (flowers, stones, bones) and the desert surrounding her house in Santa Fé, where she lived from 1949 onwards. Her identity as a woman was no less famous, immortalized as it was by her husband's photographs. She was a tiny and powerful figure with a penetrating gaze and silver hair gathered at the nape of her neck. She always wore black clothing: the only reminders of her body's existence in this all-enveloping dark wardrobe were the pieces of Indo-American jewellery that stood out powerfully against it.

OLD-FASHIONED a. Referring to things or institutions that belong to the past, or that show evident traces of deterioration and wear and tear. Person who defends the past or aesthetics prior to the electrical age. Averse to western culture because of the aesthetic damage caused by the birth of modernity, Yunichiro Tanizaki ends his *In Praise of Shadows* with an illuminating eulogy of the past: 'I would have the eaves and the walls dark, I would push back into the shadows the things that come forward too clearly, [...] perhaps we may be allowed at least one mansion where we can turn off the electric lights and see what it is like without them.' (Leete's Island Books, 1977, p. 42).

OPAQUE a. Not transmitting light, not transparent or translucent, dull. Hard to understand, unintelligible.

IRVING PENN (New Jersey, NY, 1917). American painter, graphic artist and photographer. An eminent and outstanding figure in advertising, portraiture and in fashion (his pages for *Vogue* and collaboration with editor/art director Alexander Liberman and fashion editor Diana Vreeland have gone down in history). An important defendent of multiethnicity through his work. Penn is the master of contrast and depth in black-and-white photography. Today his work is still looked up to by younger generations as a significant technical and stylistic reference point.

PHILOSOPHIC a. Indicating thought that is theoretical, practical, logical, logical-symbolic, methodological, epistemological, cosmological, metaphysical, ontological, gnosiological, theological, anthropological, psychological, ethical, political, sociological, pedagogical, etc.

PHOTOCOPY n. A photographic reproduction, produced by machine, of images or written documents on light-sensitive paper.

PHOTOGRAPHY n. The invention of Louis Jacques Mandé Daguerre's first daguerrotype, a sheet of copper coated with a light-sensitive emulsion, is estimated to have taken place between 1837 and 1839. The very origin of photography is light and dark, as well as its having first manifested itself in black and white. Among art forms it is possibly the most adapted to demonstrating how light is born from the dark. Looking at the work of various artists, from Giacomelli's observations to the shadowy exquisitely Sicilian figures of Biasiucci and Sellerio, or Capelli and Buscarino's images (a columnist and interpreter of Kantor's theatre), what stands out in their photographic interpretation is the dimension of the colour black. The black of black and white, rather than just being a simple means of expression, is a complete and separate spiritual category. The black-and-white image was destined to document and also poeticize never-to-be-repeated moments in time and is closest to being a mythology in its own right. This can be seen throughout its history, from Henri Cartier-Bresson through to Mapplethorpe, from fashion reporting through to S/M portraiture and still life photography; and from photography as a specialized language to photography as an artist's tool (for further reading *q.v.* Avedon, B/W, Black Photography, Lindbergh, Meisel, Mulas, Penn, Weber).

POLISHED a. Said of smooth objects which shine in the light.

PROFOUND a. Penetrating to a great depth, situated far from the surface. Reaching to or stemming from the depths of one's nature. Inevitably it falls upon the colour black to best illustrate the feeling of profundity, especially when used to create optical illusions. From a general and particularly visual point of view, black never fails in any of its fields of representation. A person dressed in black will seem profound, just as an emphasis on black furnishing will appear profound. Profoundness, as the mysterious and inscrutable side of the colour black, is without doubt a quality borrowed from Oriental and African cultures and transplanted into Western sensibilities (*q.v.* chador, kohl, kimono, haori, etc.) 'A glistening black lacquer rice cask set off in a dark corner is both beautiful to behold and a powerful stimulus to the appetite. When the lid is briskly lifted, and this pure white freshly boiled food, heaped in its black container, each and every grain gleaming like a pearl, sends forth billows of warm steam – here is a sight no Japanese can fail to be moved by.' (from Junichiro Tanizaki, *In Praise of Shadows*, Leete's Island Books, 1977, p. 16–7).

PULP n. An English term for something that has been reduced to mush, but also something turbid. Pulp has lent its name to a narrative style, fanzines and B-movies in which horror moves from a grim late Gothic into paradox. Violence in black humour.

PUNK n. Literally something that is rotten, insignificant, valueless. The expression later gave rise to one of the most important youth movements in the last twenty years. Chosen advocates of this phenomenon were Malcolm McLaren (strategist) and Vivienne Westwood (the creator of a look in which trashiness is the basis of provocation. A fortuitous aesthetic inspired by Sid Vicious). The myth and a vaguely accurate, ironic biographical history of the Sex Pistols (the movement's No. 1 band) can be seen in *The Great Rock 'n' Roll Swindle*, a film created and directed by McLaren. As everyone knows, the black leathers, worn tartan, tawdry 'n' sexy underclothes, and the contemptuous, anarchic and nihilistic attitudes brought notoriety to a phenomenon that, since it came out (1974–5) has affected the fashion of our time. Punk's black look has inspired fashion all over the world, from Japan to England to France and Italy. The colour is a fundamental part of the eruption of a deconstructivist, asymmetric, existentialist and dramatic look, the look of breaking away from what was before.

ANDRÉE PUTMAN (Paris, 1925). Designer. 'At the beginning I was criticized for an excessive use of black. People would say to me "you are responsible for the invasion of black ...". To boot, I worked in a predominantly black office! That was in the eighties. I think that in my case black actually means a return to white impastos, to cleanliness, to clarity, to simplicity and to austerity.' Putman, renowned in international design from France to the United States, became the leading practitioner of neominimalist interiors, from which she abolished all colours besides black, white and tones in between the two. Choosing to follow in the path of sacred monsters like Le Corbusier, Mallet-Stevens or Eileen Gray, she has designed interiors that are more like works of art owing to the high conceptual quality of her work and the extraordinary way in which she combines form and space. 'Whoever likes colour,' points out the designer, 'must love black as a jewel case that contains them all. It is like a cure, a sort of concentration within oneself, the opposite of a white sheet of paper, which is the synonym of liberty. Like any abuse of creativity, too much black is also a mistake. Today I think the main threat to black comes from Purgatory.' Not without humour but with a rigorously auto-critical eye, Putman holds some absolute and unshakeable convictions about the fundamental power of the colour black. She summarizes them with observations like: 'There is no black blacker than the veils worn by Arab women in the desert, or than the hair of the Japanese.' Or: 'Children whose mothers dress in black have more imagination than children whose mothers wear colours.'

AD REINHARDT (Buffalo, 1913 – New York, 1967). Artist. He is closely associated with the birth and spread of monochrome painting and is considered to be one of the instigators of Minimalist art. After his abstract paintings of the thirties, clearly influenced by Indian and Arab decorative art, and the interest then focused on Oriental calligraphy, in the fifties Reinhardt came to geometric installations. These were almost monochrome right from the start, for instance, his *Red Paintings*. They harmonize in their rigorous progression of minimal tonal variations, played out in tones of green, brown and violet (*Black Paintings*). His intention was clearly to transcend (with rigour on the one hand and mysticism on the other), the two-dimensional quality of a painting.

RIGOUR–RIGOROUS 1. n. 2. a. Inspired by minimalist and conceptual art, 'rigour' and 'rigorous' are the terms most often applied to works of impeccable geometry characterized by monochrome colour choices like black and white, which reveal the author's intention to efface the more tangible and concrete aspects of art. This concept goes against the possibile ostentation of an art object, and rigorously black works represent the first step, for artists like Robert Morris, Donald Judd, Sol LeWitt or Joseph Kosuth, towards underlining the priority of the intellectual and the conceptual, instead of the purely perceptive pleasure of a work. Definitions like 'rigour' and 'rigorous', referring to black and white, were at the height of their fame in the sixties and seventies, but have slowly fallen into disuse, having shown their semantic limitations.

RITUAL a. Of or relating to a rite, pertaining to a ceremony. In general terms, the ensemble of norms that regulate a rite.

ROCK'N'ROLL n. A product of post-war America, inspired by black musical culture (jazz, blues, soul), rock is one of the languages that has been most successful in establishing complicity and communication between blacks and whites. Landmarks include Elvis Presley's film *Rock Around the Clock* and the birth of the Motown recording label, which for the first time brought a series of predominantly black bands and solo artists to an international public. Artists include the Jackson Five and Ike and Tina Turner. Particular homage must be paid to the great innovations of artists like Little Richard, Chick Corea, John Coltrane, Louis Armstrong, etc. who introduced new developments in both jazz and rock. Rock'n'roll means glamour: skin-tight clothing and black leather, like the carefully elaborated outfits adopted by the Hell's Angels, a community of nomadic bikers; like the jackets worn by the beautiful and the damned, James Dean and Marlon Brando.

SONIA RYKIEL (Paris, 1930). Fashion stylist by trade, she started to design garments for herself when she was pregnant. The queen of knitwear, drawing basically on the functional and transgressive traditions of Chanel and Schiaparelli, she makes patchwork designs in angora, mohair and other soft wools. Like her forerunners, Rykiel has also built up an unmistakable and charismatic personal image over time. Her frizzy red hair, cut in a pyramid-shape, stands out against the fantastically pale skin of her expressive, mask-like face. The rest of her, invariably covered in very long, fluid and inevitably black knitwear, remains in the shadow.

S/M n. Short for sadomasochism: the coexistence of sadistic and masochistic tendencies in the same person. Perversion and cruelty for its own sake, which is manifested in a desire to inflict pain on others and in pleasure in being the object of pain inflicted on the self by others.

YVES SAINT LAURENT (Oran, Algeria, 1936). Fashion designer. At age 17 he won first prize in a fashion competition with a cocktail dress. He was later employed by Dior, stepping into the great designer's shoes when Dior died four years later. His designs were immediately different, provocative, flying in the face of the trends of the time and the tastes of the New Look's creator. 1958 brought us the trapeze; 1960 black leather jackets – the first time that street fashion hit the catwalks; 1963 thigh-length boots; 1965 art drawn into fashion with dresses inspired by Mondrian; 1966 dinner jackets or tuxedos for women; in 1969 trouser suits and in 1971 the blazer. Saint Laurent was the king of fashion throughout the seventies, when his creations increasingly drew on ethnic inspiration. He invented a casual yet infinitely elegant style of dress which reflects the spirit of the times: from black cocktail dresses to lingerie lace for his nude-look outfits.

SEDUCTION n. The capacity to fascinate.

SHADOW n. A reduction in light, owing to an opaque body placed between the source of light and the body or zone to be illuminated. Dark pattern projected by any opaque form that is exposed to a light source. Indistinct shape, enveloped in darkness. Ghost, spectre, spirit. An unclear element or detail that is a source of misunderstanding, suspicion or fear.

SILHOUETTE n. A profile or the clearly-defined outline of an object filled with black ink. It can also be a portrait in profile cut out of black paper. In contemporary language it is also used to describe the lines or shape of an item of fashion clothing.

JUNICHIRO TANIZAKI (Tokyo, 1886–1965). Novelist. Born into a wealthy family, at the age of seventeen he was forced to make a living as a private tutor after his family's financial ruin. The unexpected events awoke him to literature, and he had early success with stories published in the school magazine. He applied to Tokyo University to study in the Faculty of Letters, failed to get his degree and was expelled for not paying his fees. He was at the opposite end of the scale and in conflict with the literary movements of his time – naturalism and *Shishosetsu* ('The novel of the I') in which the presence of the author dominates the narrative – and joined an opposition group founding with them *Subaru*, *Mita Bunkagu* and *Shirakaba* magazines. He thus helped to fuel the birth of a literary genre dubbed by the Japanese (great pigeonholers) as 'diabolic', creating a link and elective affinities with westerners like Poe, Wilde and Baudelaire. Sadism, sensuality and active masochism without a doubt make Tanizaki a dark writer, whose fantasies are often heavily censored. The essay '*In'ei raisan*' (1933), translated as *In Praise of Shadows* is considered to be his masterpiece. Hovering between irony and regret, the author upholds the superiority of oriental sensitivity ('world of shadow') to the detriment of Western sensitivity ('world of light'), by examining different objects and inventions. His shadowy world is evocative without being explicit. Darkness is sovereign: like ladies' veils in former times, its appeal is irresistible.

TATTOO n. A permanent drawing derived from the tradition of body paintings. It consists of cutting into the skin and using certain substances to slow down the healing process, or injecting the skin with substances that will colour it.

PHILIP TREACY (London, 1963). Millinery designer. For Philip Treacy the hat is a fashion object in itself. It lives and communicates from above, like an intelligent being with the ability to overcome the identity and wrest away the authority of the human being wearing it. Like every good Englishman, Treacy considers the crown to be an historic and ineluctable complement to tradition, a source of historic events which are inevitably to be found transcribed in gossip columns and from gossip turn into fiction, to pure creativity. No brakes, no limits. In the name of pure abstraction, his ironically and sophisticatedly authoritarian, invasive, genial and capricious hats assume a dominant bearing. They are a magnificent and pompous spectacle, homage paid to the surreal side of existence. They are sculptures that reproduce all the paradoxes of aristocratic culture. They are works of a groundbreaking nature whose state of grace is impudence (translated from Mariuccia Casadio, 'Philip Treacy' in *Visitors*, by Luigi Settembrini and Franca Sozzani, Florence Biennial, Skira, 1996).

CY TWOMBLY (Lexington, Virginia, 1929). Painter. After travelling across Italy as a young man (1951–2), Twombly returned to Rome to settle in 1957. He belongs to an atypical category of artists, although he is often associated with Rauschenberg, Kline or Motherwell. His technique can be described, in synthesis, as a combination of elegant, intricate and primary graphics which combine numbers, Latin inscriptions and abstract signs scratched onto often dark, monochrome surfaces like blackboards.

UNIFORM n. An outfit that is common to all the members of a clan, association or confraternity. The ensemble of garments that have to be worn according to set rules.

JAMES VAN DER ZEE (Lenox, Mass., 1886 – New York, 1983). The first great Afro-American photographer of this century, and one of the most important masters of photography in general. His career lasted over eighty years, starting with portraits of his family and friends in Lenox, where he grew up, and concluding with marvellous portraits of, among others, Bing Crosby, Eubie Blake and Jean Michel Basquiat. His reputation was, however, built on the thousands of photos he took in Harlem, New York, between the two world wars.

GIANNI VERSACE (Reggio Calabria, 1946 – Miami, 1997). Fashion designer. Curious about everything, passionate about haute couture, but also about art, archeology, dance, theatre and cinema, Gianni Versace was unique in the world of fashion. Creator of a refined and at the same time sexy, feminine look, he was also the founder of a radically original conception of male fashion. His was and is a modern look, where men show their desire, vanity and strong sexuality. He was internationally respected and acclaimed. An exhibition at the Costume Institute of the Metropolitan Museum of New York was recently dedicated to his collections. He was of unsurpassed inventiveness and an innovator of the concept of glamour. He was a myth in the world of megastars, who often turned to his ideas and advice to build themselves new identities and wardrobes. Richard Martin (Director of the Costume Institute at the Metropolitan) considers his use of black studded leather, his designs in metal mesh and his prints to be an important contribution to the collective imagination.

VICTORIAN a. Denominating the style inspired by Victoria, Queen of England from 1837 until 1901. Although she was not the most elegant dresser, Queen Victoria's decision to adopt severe mourning dress after the death of her husband in 1860 (Albert of Saxe-Coburg-Gotha, whom she married in 1840), had some considerable influence on female fashion in England. Dressed in black from head to toe, from her dress (the production of black cloth shot to historic heights in those years), to her jewellery (granite and jet), to her collar and the baubles on her hat, Queen Victoria brought in a fashion that, however monochrome, was far from sober. With her stiff, quasi-masculine, charismatic allure, she ended up seducing overseas noblewomen as well, who where often puritan but vain, lacking in taste but of ample means which they freely deployed ordering the latest in mourning dresses from Paris and London.

LUCHINO VISCONTI (Milan 1906 – Rome, 1976). Film director. Met Gide, Bernstein and Cocteau in Paris. In 1936, through his friend Coco Chanel, he met Jean Renoir. This meeting was decisive for the impetuous young Milanese nobleman. He was Renoir's assistant and costumier in the film *Une partie de campagne*. In Italy he frequented the anti-fascist intelligentsia and sold his mother's jewellery to produce his first film, the neorealist *Ossessione*. A free interpretation of American writer James Cain's novel *The Postman Always Rings Twice*, this début film is also a very personal essay in black-and-white film-making techniques, which here acquire the same tragic notes of impossible love that inspire the subject matter. 'Black is the colour of beauty par excellence,' observed the film director. His use of black-and-white in the 1948 film *La terra trema*, inspired by the social realism of Verga's *I Malavoglia*, is as elegant as it is sober. He had the opportunity to work with Anna Magnani on the set of *Bellissima*, a Cesare Zavattini film, which he transformed into one of the most moving examples of Italian neorealism. No less memorable is his film *Rocco e i suoi fratelli*, only recently discovered by the American public along with Visconti's atypical and eclectic style. Today Visconti can be placed without hesitation on the list of cult film directors of world renown, as an excellent representative of a shadowy and decadent aesthetic inspired by the literature of Dostoevsky, Camus and Mann, and the music of composers like Wagner or Verdi.

DIANA VREELAND (Paris 1906 – New York 1988). After 25 years as Fashion Editor of *Harper's Bazaar* (from 1939) she joined Condé Nast, directing *Vogue* for them until 1972. An unrivalled figure in the fashion world, she was the author of an intuitive and evocative, decidedly artistic rapport with the fashion pages. She formed the professional sensibilities of photographers like Penn or Avedon as well as foreshadowing the contemporary identity of top models through her collaboration with Marisa Berenson, Jean Schrimpton, Twiggy and Verushka. In 1973 she became Director of The Costume Institute of the Metropolitan Museum of New York. Her exhibitions have gone down in history as an expression and synthesis of her multiethnic, epoch-swallowing sensibilities, rich with artistic references to fashion. With her patrimony of ideas about progress, convictions and suggestions on fashion, reflected coherently in her choices in life and her appearance, Vreeland has become a kind of icon. To her inexhaustible flock of adepts and cultivators she has symbolized both vitality and the more valuable aspects of decadence in her systematic, timeless and consistent use of colours and unquestionable choice of simple lines and impeccable cuts. Famous for her unexpected and inspired declarations on fashion, Vreeland has several times discussed the charismatic power of black. Timeless are comments like: 'I'd like to be luxuriously dressed. I'd like to have on the most luxurious black cashmere sweater, the most luxurious black satin pants.'

BRUCE WEBER (Greensburg, Pennsylvania, 1946). Photographer. His professional origins lie between the pages of *Interview* (in the Warhol seventies) and Condé Nast covers in Italy and the USA. A talent scout and supreme, on-the-road discoverer of talent in the making, Weber is extremely sensitive to contemporary beauty. He records it and spreads the word, capturing every nuance of gesture and expression. Gifted with a subtle and original artistic flair, he knows how to translate life into art and art into life, as can be seen in the extremely natural and fluid narrative of his black and white photography.

YOHJI YAMAMOTO (Japan, 1943). Fashion designer. Graduated from Tokyo's Keio University (1966) and then studied at the Bunka College of Fashion before opening his business in 1972. First collection shown in 1976. The creator of deconstructed forms, moulded clothing made of enormous, miraculously seamless swathes of cloth, Yamamoto is, along with Rei Kawakubo, one of the most radical and innovative voices of contemporary fashion. With his initial fusion of East and West, the synthetic archaism derived from his own culture combined with the provocative superabundance of London, Paris and US street-fashion language (anything from proto-punk to New Wave), Yamamoto affirms the essential and irreplaceable power of black. Black is a not only a recurring presence, but also a point of departure and a main thread running through his work, although he cyclically links it to radiant and gaudy colours that are no less emphatic, as if he were throwing down the gauntlet before current colour metaphors.

ZONE (*q.v.* Shadow). In this case, all that still seems obscure after you have read this glossary. Or also, all that, for reasons of space and time, we have missed or have been obliged to omit.

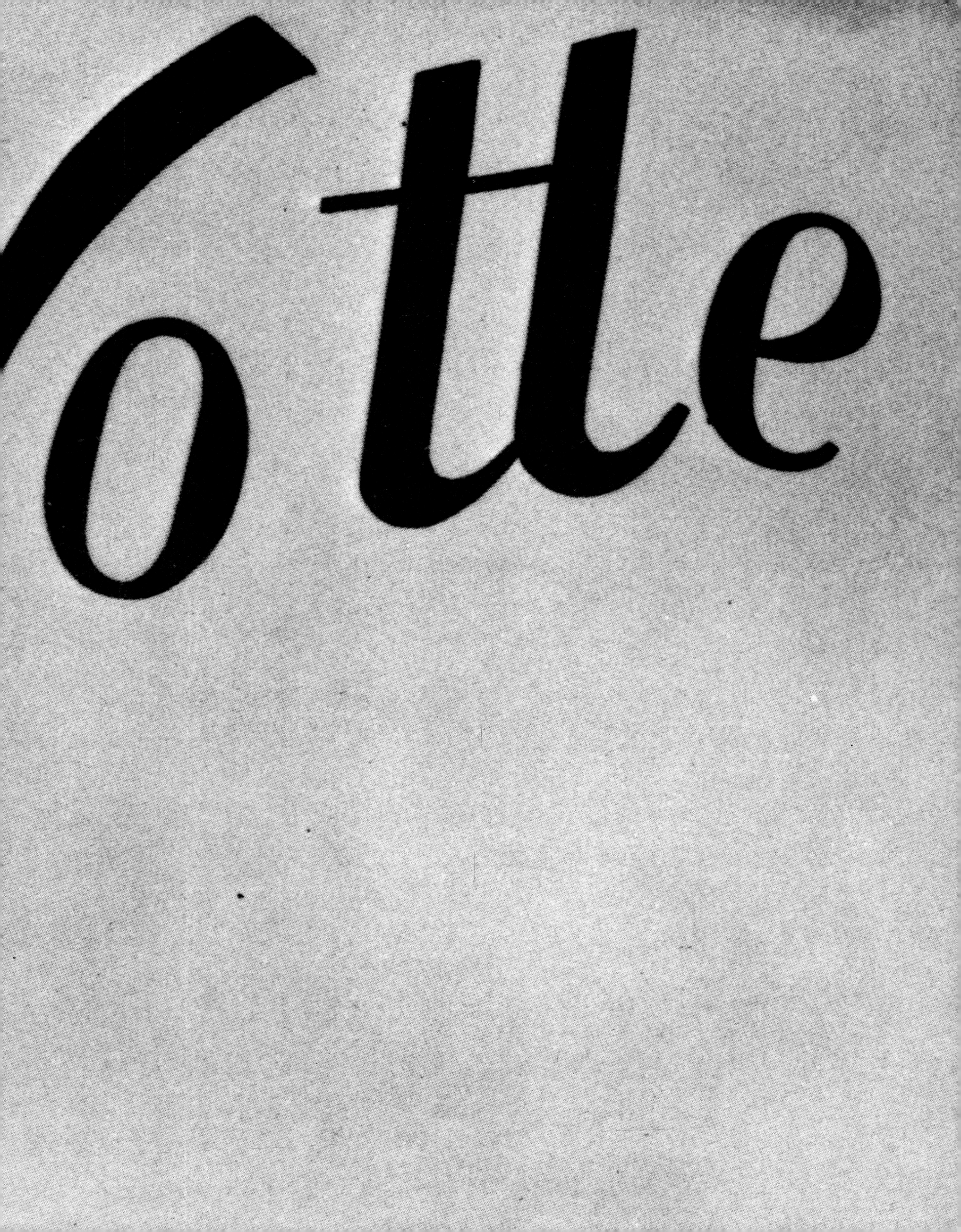
otle

In 1925 Paris was prostrated adoringly at the feet of a black Venus, Josephine Baker. She was an American dancer and singer, born to a very poor Mississippi family who had emigrated back to the Old World to seek their fortune, a journey made in the opposite direction to that taken in those days by so many Europeans. Once in Paris, she immediately became the star performer in Sissin's *Black Revue*. She used to sing 'Yes, we have no bananas,' wearing no more than a little skirt made of bananas. It was not long before she had been right around Europe, wildly applauded on one tour after another. Seventy years later, the Paris fashion world and, indeed, the whole world is prostrating itself before another black American Venus, Naomi Campbell. The absolute supermodel, she incarnates the end-of-century ideal of beauty. She is the only woman who is so perfect as to resemble a work of art: with her oval face and moon-shaped full lips she could have been the model used by sculptor Constantin Brancusi in the twenties to create his *Négresse*. Only Brancusi never copied from real life, but sought deep within himself (with a little input from the stylization he learnt from African art) to find the archetypal form – the state of pure beauty. Baker the day before yesterday, and Naomi today: the twentieth century opened and will close in black, having chosen two black women as its goddesses of beauty. Maybe just a coincidence in the history of fashion, but probably less a coincidence than a sign of the circular path fashion has followed over the course of the century. Throughout this time the West has returned periodically to draw on the wealth of black African expression whether in ideas, sounds or colours: the same cultures that in every other way represented primitivism and savagery – humanity in its raw and untamed state. It is this which gives these cultures their potentially dangerous sensual and seductive power. This power needed refining and neutralizing, a feat that was accomplished through the process of assimilation in the colonial era, with troops and missionary schools, segregation and ghettos. Throughout the entire century the pendulum has swung between fascination and rejection, total devotion (the '*manie nègre*' in the twenties and thirties when every Parisian intellectual's salon and every artist's atelier was overflowing with tribal sculptures, masks and fetishes – a trend started by Picasso, Tzara and Derain) and total control, and admiration mixed with contempt. In 1912 the major works of the European avant-garde, who at home were constructing a vocabulary of expression by borrowing freely from primitive African art, went to New York for an exhibition which soon made history. For us today it is comical to imagine the cognoscenti in Manhattan avidly discussing the Bantu masks in Picasso's *Demoiselles d'Avignon* or Archipenko's bronzes over the bowed heads of liveried servants who, most of them, were descended – even if remotely – from tribal cultures. It has not been easy for the West to accord dignity to the continent that it so conscientiously colonized. Black culture has not had an easy time finding a space for itself in the jungle of black stereotypes that have accumulated over at least two centuries. Blacks with their innate sense of rhythm, good at song and dance; blacks with their love of colour and heaps of oversize, dazzling, outré jewellery, whether it is the giraffe-collars of the Masai women or a Harlem rapper's cascade of rings, bracelets and chains. Black means instinct and potent sensuality – dangerously close to nature – with an eroticism that in the eighties and nineties seems to have taken hold of the gay imagination in particular, with examples like Mapplethorpe's sculpturesque models, and Carl Lewis – the incarnation of athletic perfection – who wore stilettos for a tyre commercial. Now that society's collective sensitivity has reached virtually the opposite end of the scale from what it was at the beginning of the century, these characteristics have turned into qualities. Together they propagate the dream of a black man who is still close to the gates of Eden, a man untouched by Western man's identity crisis, who is still able to draw energy from his roots, from the primary sources of life. This mythical black man probably no longer even exists now that the First World has spread its values and its dislikes all over the planet. It is a mythical state, but apparently one for which postmodern culture has a great need. There are so many areas of creativity – music, literature, fashion, cinema – which turn to the black world for ideas and energy. In the thirties and forties jazz was considered to be a 'dirty' and vulgar music, created by 'niggers' for 'niggers' in sleazy American bars. Now it is an elitist universe with a few high priests and many millions of devotees. It has inspired classical music and rock music, anything from Gershwin to Prokofiev to Sting and from being the devil's music it has become the epitome of cool – thanks to extraordinary prophets of fusion like Miles Davis. Johnny Clegg, a 'progressive' white, has founded and nourished his music on the syncopated energy of Zulu rhythms, the other face of South African culture which until recently was forbidden. Peter Gabriel, a genius of music and multimedia performances, has knocked on the ethnic door of Youssou n'Dour to record unforgettable duets. The call of black music, the irresistible attraction of a genetically transmitted sense of rhythm, was even heard in provincial Italy in the sixties, inspiring Nino Ferrer's *Vorrei la pelle nera*, and keeping a whole generation of teenagers dancing to the tune of the hully gully and dreaming of the impossible elegance of the Watutsi. This brings us back to the beauty of black peoples, the magical stereotype that has always counterbalanced, in the European unconscious, the figure of the small-statured Bushman with his squashed nose and bulbous eyes, squatting behind a bush spying on a gazelle. These are the demigods: the Masai, the Watutsi, the Zulu, the Kikuyu, the Somali, tall, slender men and women of outstanding beauty and natural elegance who look regal with no more than a brick- or saffron-coloured rag draped over their ebony skin. In reality black Africa is an explosion of colour: the colours of the feather headdresses and bead necklaces of the Masai, the colours of the cloths and painted houses of the Ndebele women. We find the same colours and the same taste for joyful, totally abandoned decoration returning from time to time to liven up the fashion world, like last year's pro-African, tribal (rather than ethnic) collections dreamt up by John Galliano for Dior. However, if black Africa displays all the colours of the rainbow, black black is the undisputed master in the African north. The black of a chador is the black of absence, invisibility and negation. It is perhaps due to the ever growing and problematic contiguity of Islam that this black holds the art of the West in the throes of a fascination that is not devoid of troubling aspects. The chador is the extreme religious and political fruit of the Arab world's love of darkness: the darkness of carved wooden shutters that conceal faces, the blackness of arcades and windshields that block out the sunlight, the darkness of henna and kohl that blackens women's eyes to emphasize their luminosity. Iranian photographer Shirin Neshat uses it in her work. Her women are always draped in black cloth and, consistent with the gloom of their garb, are carrying a weapon or rifle in their intricately hennaed hands. The dark gauze of chadors swells over slender metal stakes to become airy cocoons, suspended in the latest installations of Italian conceptual artist Chiara Dynys: this is the most frightening African black today. The mystery of equatorial forests and unexplored corners of what once was the dark continent has long since gone; today the darkness is ideological, arising from a clash of cultures. Yet Europe is still drawn to it, as if to a disaster. Europe is afraid of this darkness, yet it searches for it. It copies and is inspired by it. It spreads kohl around its eyes and hopes that light will be born from the darkness, thus unconsciously giving credence to the theories of Martin Bernal, the academic who a few years ago suggested that Greek civilization – the pillar and foundation of Western knowledge – owes a huge debt to African civilization. According to him, from Africa came the light of the logos. The bold title of his book? *Black Athens*. Elisabetta Planca.

to be b
is bea

mandela
face

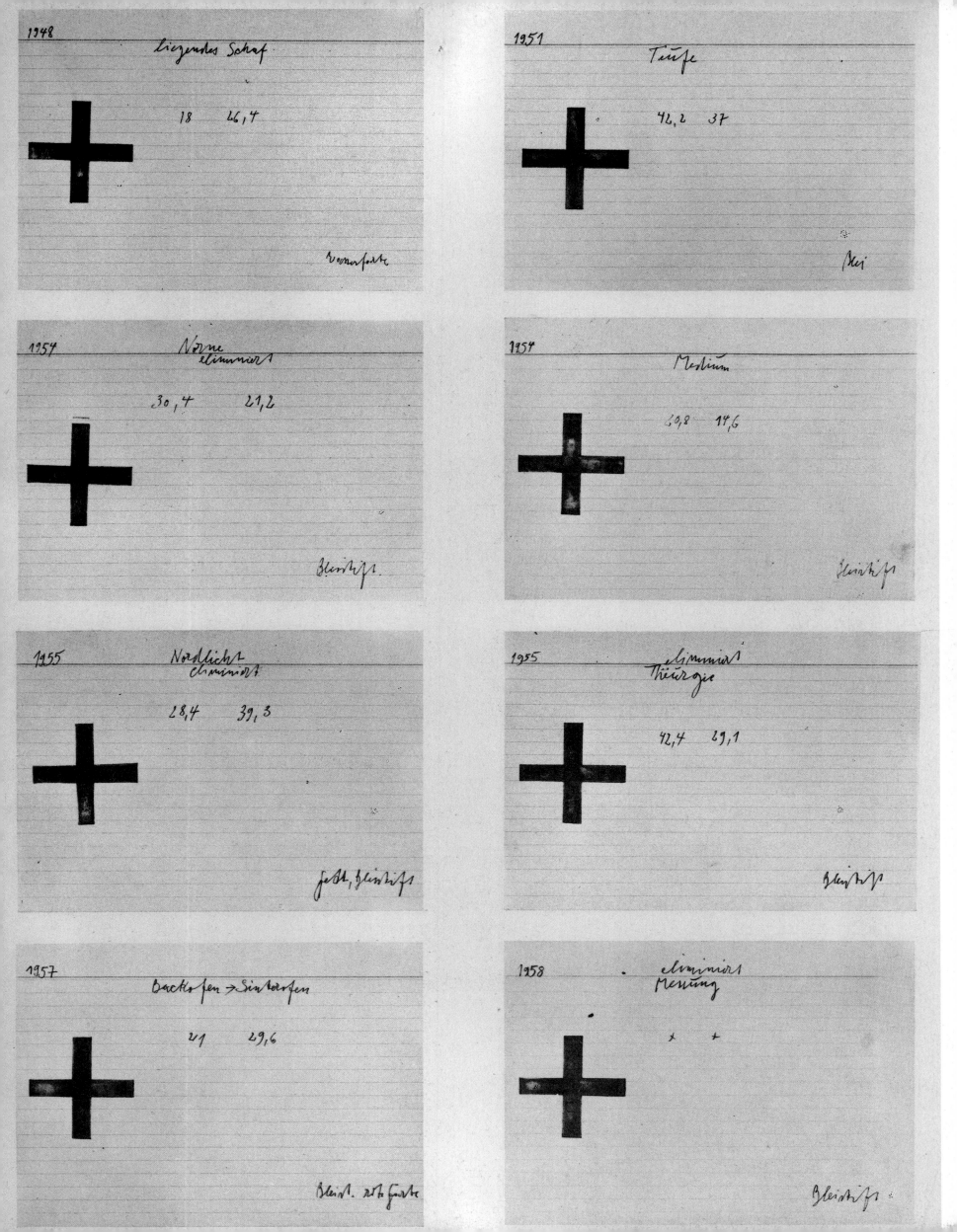

INTERNATIONALE AUSSTELLUNG BARCELONA 1929.
REPRÄSENTATIONSPAVILLON DES DEUTSCHEN REICHES

18 cm

HARTHOLZ.

18 cm

ST. STÜTZENPROFIL M 1:1
MANTELBLECHE (VERNICKELT)

Nº 27

1929.

К. МАЛЕВИЧЪ.

ОТЪ КУБИЗМА И ФУТУРИЗМА == == КЪ СУПРЕМАТИЗМУ.

НОВЫЙ ЖИВОПИСНЫЙ
◆ ◆ РЕАЛИЗМЪ. ◆ ◆

ИЗДАНІЕ ТРЕТЬЕ.

МОСКВА.

1916.

VIRTUE

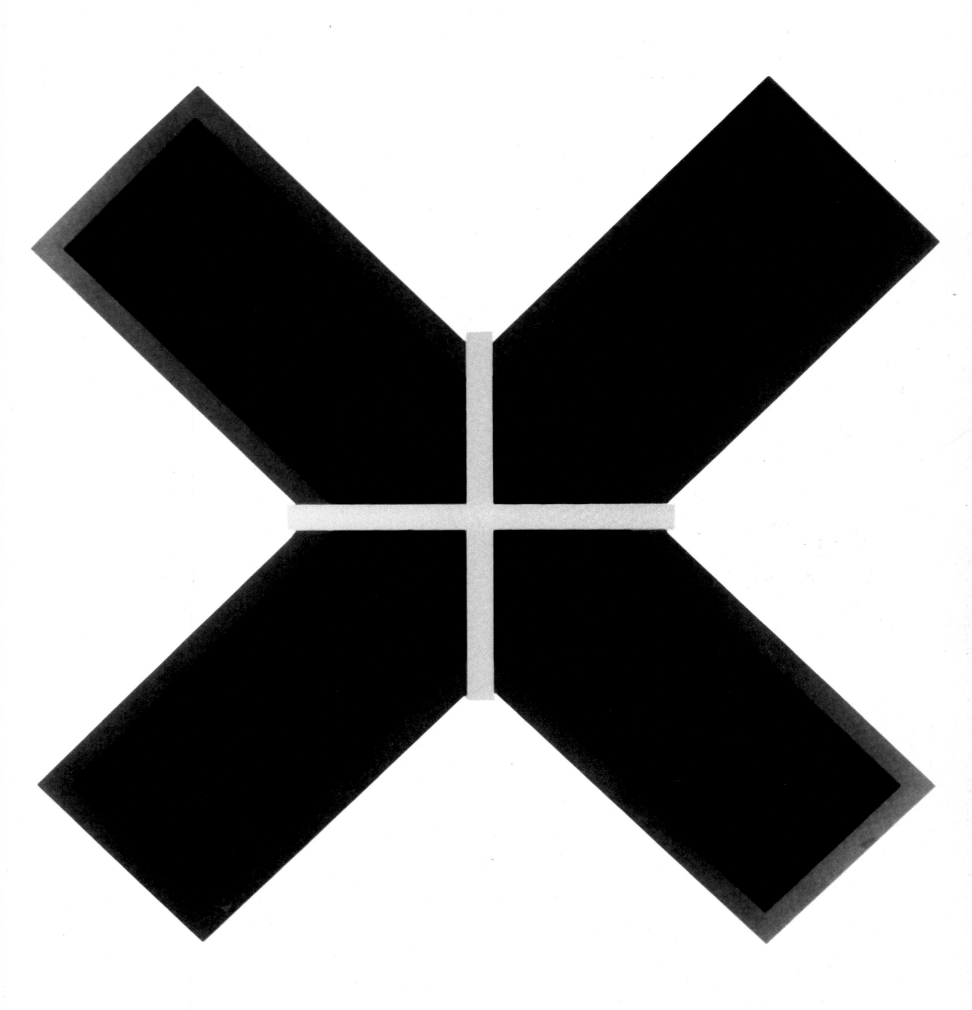

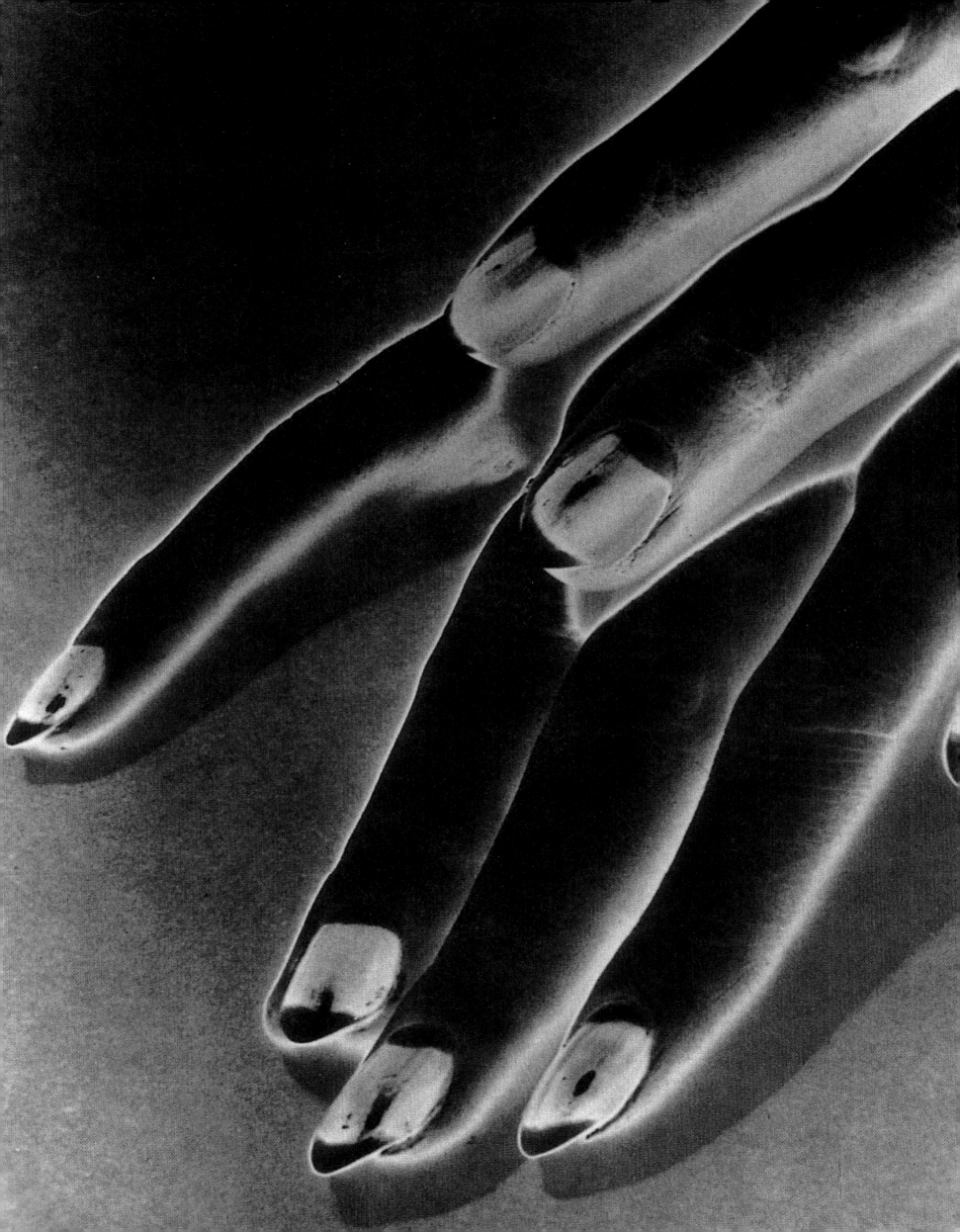

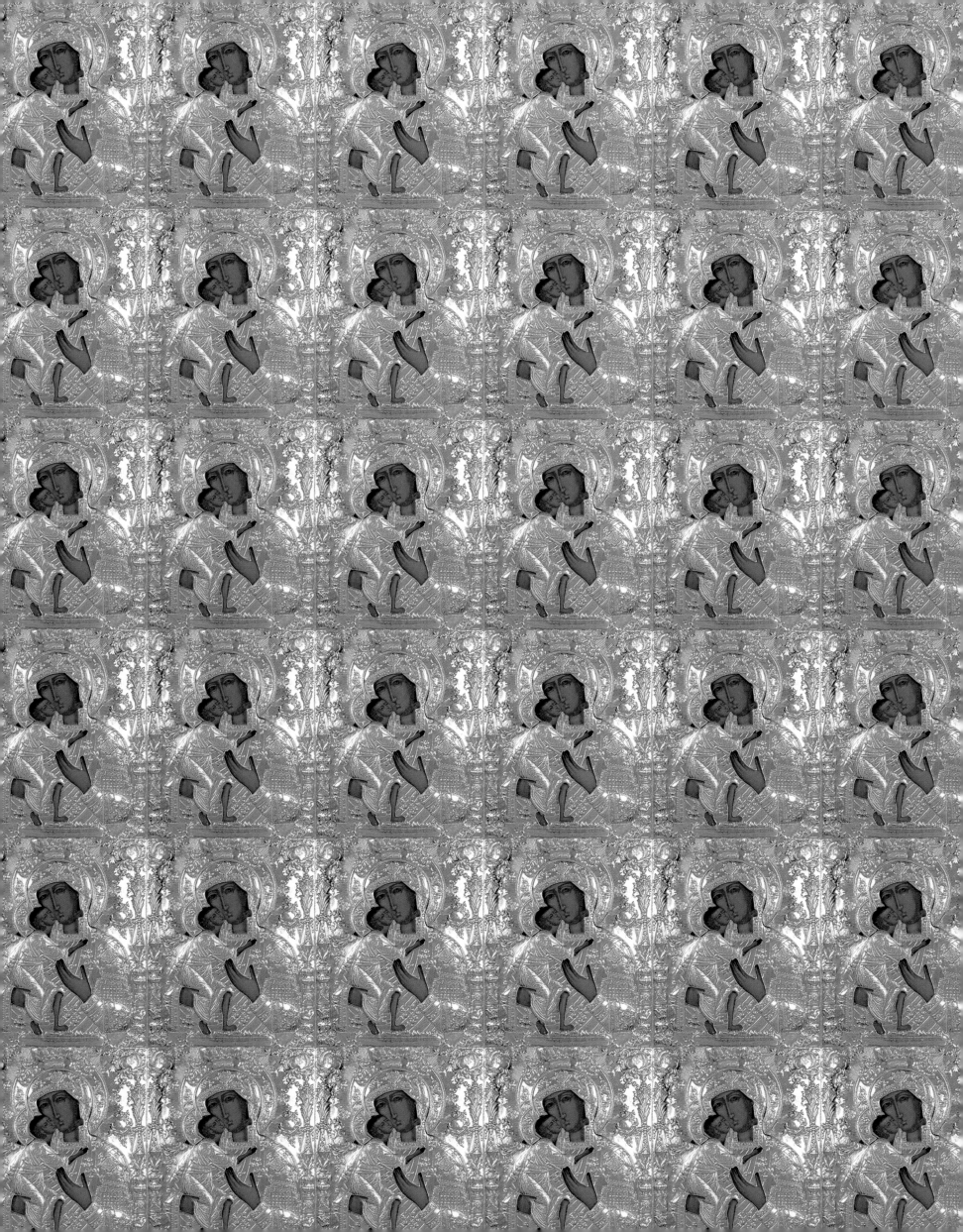

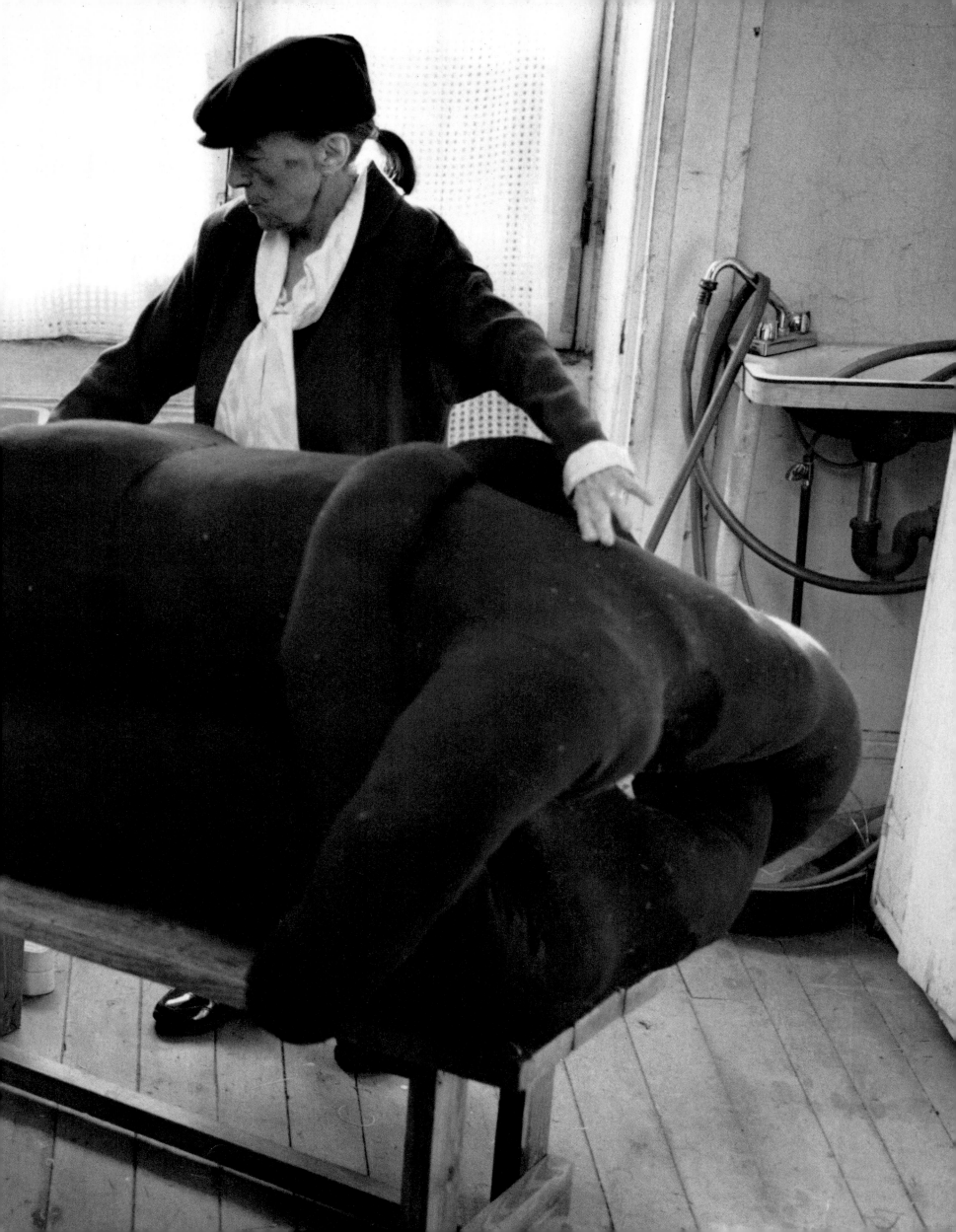

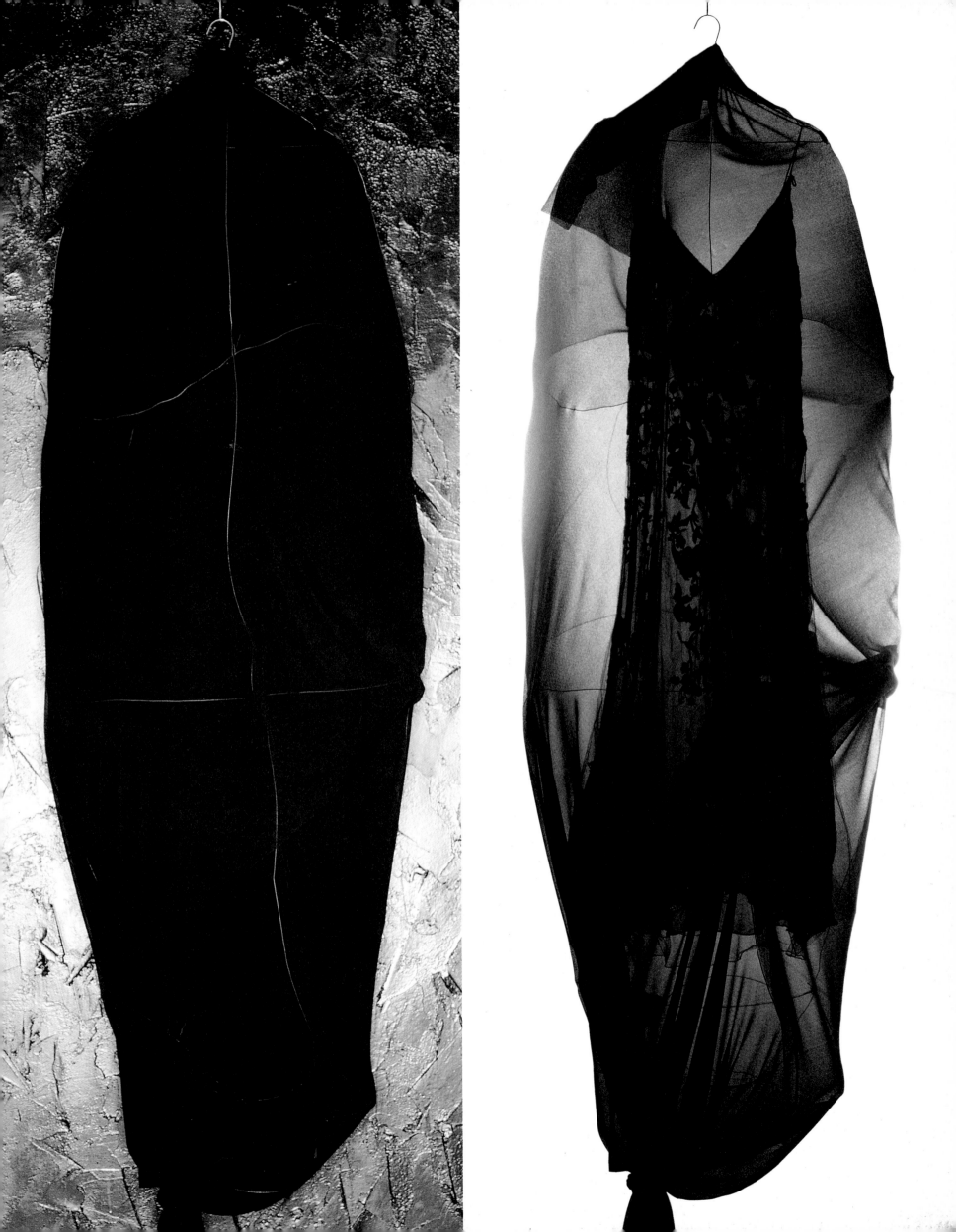

It is rigorous yet emphatic, radical yet romantic, ancient, yet continually repeated and readapted by modern culture: like white, black is not a colour but needs all colours to exist. Unlike white, it has a tendency to emphasize contours and volumes. It underlines the impact and weight of a form in the same way white erases it, makes it invisible, light, even ghostly. It is no surprise that the most theoretic and conceptual images in art have been created by the interplay of these opposites. They have been the means of expression of the most provocative, spectacular and surprising work, which has often remained unpublished. The twentieth century can be summed up as an alternation between emptiness and plenitude, between eradication and revision, reaching a symbolic climax in monochrome painting and later carrying out a voiding of space and the disappearance of the object. In the process, black, a far more direct, spectacular and provocative colour than white, provided the bridge between the fullness favoured by the West, and the Oriental use of the void. It emphasizes the most disturbing and seductive characteristics of darkness, with a range of indefinably dark tones that culminate in total black. It creates conditions favourable to introspective hallucinations, or to virtual and temporal alterations related to the dimensions of space and time. It is the ultimate contrast with the undefinedness, weakness or lack of precision of the inks or figures that surround it and for which it acts as a frame. It can dominate, impinge on, impose on, or highlight each shape or object, sign or action, and turn them into the main protagonist at the very moment its properties are called into play. There is no doubt about its endless resources. They are a constant source of inspiration to the art world, which in turn inspires the worlds of fashion and interior design to find its most original and fascinating solutions, whether from the point of view of stylistic rigour or with regard to the most extreme aspects of sensuality or suggestiveness imaginable, or, in general, what character to give form, matter and volume in virtue of or as a consequence of their dominant colour. It is thanks to the gift of being able to absorb and synthesize into itself all other existing colours that black, without providing continuity, becomes a metaphor that links the end to the beginning, death to life and night to day. Black is black, indifferent to other, external effects of light or dark. In situations of extreme contrast or total mimesis, shapes can affirm a kind of final and immutable nature through the colour black. Rimbaud's composition, 'Les Voyelles', is now a part of the history of poetry. Black appears in the first verse, not by coincidence, linked to the vowel 'A'. The poet then extrapolates a profoundly feminine, morbid and cruel vision of the colour: 'A, noir corset velu des mouches éclatantes/ Qui bombinent autour des puanteurs cruelles,/ Golfes d'ombre'. [A. Black, hairy corset of blatant flies /

Splurging around cruel stenches / Gulfs of darkness.] This image alone is sufficient to establish black as the colour of female sexuality, a colour indeed favoured by most women involved in modern and contemporary art. Black plays a major part in the work of powerful personalities, for instance the monumental sculptures of artists like Louise Nevelson or Louise Bourgeois. Black works to preserve the physical nature and weight of materials that are traditionally worked with a hammer and chisel, for instance, marble, wood or stone, or cast, like bronze, into disposable clay and wax moulds and finished off with a file and soldering iron. This process has been the artistic stamp of these two cardinal figures of twentieth-century American culture. They have never lost their interest in the mysterious and imposing power of the colour black. It has helped tell the tale of two different, important and very disturbing adventures of the senses: for Nevelson black was the sole protagonist in her work, except when she contrasted it with white. Bourgeois used it along with light, transparent, inconsistent glass and the disturbing, insurmountable metallic barriers of grilles from concentration camps. It can also be said that black is the colour of female memory. This can be seen on both sides of the Atlantic, with artists like Rebecca Horn and Rosemarie Trockel, Annette Lemieux and Annette Messager. We can see both shapes in their work which are at the same time defensive and alarming — even threatening. Recovered objects like a grand piano or the archetypal typewriter; the use of bronze or the use of cloth, hand-sewn coloured fetishes; a passion for ostrich feathers or for soldiers' helmets — all are metaphorical defences against the violence of the outside world and the masculine minds which conceived them. Other examples that show the fragile and protective nature of this non-colour colour are Rebecca Horn's adoption of a black mask to eliminate, along with the sense of sight, a certain preconceived connection between the external aspect of things and their essence. James Lee Byers incorporated a mask-bandanna into what is an alchemist's wardrobe of constant monochrome, and so made a niche for himself in our contemporary consciousness and knowledge. These examples are material as well as symbolic, and unpredictably 'different' from the categorical and concentrating characteristics that are generally given to the colour. Further to this, black is linked to costume, both in ethnic culture and as a frame for the cataloguing or classification of different styles. It is also seen as an object, and as meaning reduced to its most essential features. In Joseph Beuys' blackboards and Joseph Kosuth's epistemological panels, we see work that is built on a policy of the total negation of colour. The work of these artists is used as a stand for white captions, characteristic revisions or reflections linked to the conceptual period in art of the sixties and seventies. Their negation of

colour can be seen in the attempt to reduce to a minimum the strength of expression and material appeal of the work in favour of an aesthetic identity boiled down to just black and white. The work seems to be dedicated to pure philosophical contemplation and conceived as an antithesis to misleading, decorative visual pleasure. The latter is based on market and consumer logic, which distances us relentlessly from the original and fundamental meaning of 'art for art's sake'. Following the notes bar by bar in these aesthetically rigorous scores, black was used as an elegant backdrop, support and commentator cataloguing the starched collars and post literam pop objects signed by New York artists McDermott and McGough. Having taken a step backwards in poetic time, the two are leading figures in an art and lifestyle that have been back-dated one hundred years. With scrupulous accuracy they are rewriting contemporary art from a pre-modern and pre-electric point of view, sporadically bringing back monochrome black or white, but also combining the two to remind us of the unsurpassed charm of tails and starched shirts, top hats and spats: the supremely elegant, if somewhat monochrome, appearance of collective life at the origins of bourgeois culture. German artist Georg Herold is no less ironic, Indo-British artist Anish Kapoor is no less of an alchemist. The use of recycled objects or pure pigments in powder form invest the apparently inexhaustible tale of black in the twentieth century with new and vital energy. They have paid homage to the banality of Western dress: the black handbags favoured by air stewardesses and church-going grannies are given a new lease of life, left lying open and full of gravel to underline the obscure semantics of the authors. Or the same bag can be seen closed, with its clasp gripped in a vice, suggesting its safe-box connotations, an ironic hint at the stupidity of fear as an end in itself. Among the very recent icons produced by the new generations of international artists the provocative presence of the feminine in response to the backward-looking culture of Islamic fundamentalism cannot be ignored. An Iranian artist now living in New York, Shirin Neshat, creates self-portraits as a support to cultural memories in which the colour black is noticeably dominant. She ably translates her passivity into a disturbing message of strength, aggression against and transgression of the conventionally imposed canons of her tradition. Behind the veil, the ritual henna skin decoration, the possibility of showing small parts of facial expressions and the shape of hands and feet, there is a route to liberty. Or perhaps the possibility to turn oppression into violence, with the same placid, inexpressive immutability imposed on and accepted by Muslim women. This brief history of the colour black in art could go much further and reveal other no less appealing conceptual and aesthetic properties, yet we already have at our fingertips a vast potential of variables which (as is not always the

case) have a twofold quality. On the one hand they allow us to view the 'classic' aspects of modern art, and on the other these variables show us their timeless ability to regenerate and update their own significance. Without ever repeating itself, and always there at the limits of artistic possibility, black can inspire an agonizing sense of nostalgia and at the same time produce profoundly poetic perceptions in the contemporary world. Its dual power of erasure and emphasis is what provides this juxtaposition of ineradicable memories and a radically innovative quest for the new. This is suggested with great sensitivity in Japanese writer Junichiro Tanizaki's *In Praise of Shadows*. Originally intended as a homage to the seductive power of Japan in the age before electricity, the book concludes with recognition of the irreversible fall from grace that the country has suffered. Nevertheless it leaves open and in the hands of Art the possibility to keep alive all that is dark. All that is protected by shadows, lost in the folds of unfathomable mysteries – mysterious due to its invisible, elusive, ambiguous, precious nature. The encounter between East and West, as identified by Tanizaki, has changed more than just the expressive tradition of Japanese style. Far greater conclusions may be drawn, reading between the lines: the change has been reciprocal, radical, even painful, but not without becoming a source of new hybridizations and inspiration. 'Japan has chosen', Tanizaki writes, 'to follow the West, and there is nothing for her to do but move bravely ahead and leave us old ones behind. But we must be resigned to the fact that as long as our skin is the color it is the loss we have suffered cannot be remedied. I have written all this because I thought that there might still be somewhere, possibly in literature or the arts, where something could be saved. I would call back at least for literature this world of shadows we are losing. In the mansion called literature I would have the eaves deep and the walls dark, I would push back into the shadows the things that come forward too clearly, I would strip away the useless decaration. I do not ask that this be done everywhere, but perhaps we may be allowed at least one mansion where we can turn off the electric lights and see what it is like without them.' (Leete's Island Books, 1977, p. 42). Let us try to understand these lines as a metaphor of the relationship between life and art, art in the past and art yet to come, between tradition and progress and between ideas and objects. We will be told as a warning that black belongs irrevocably to the myth of style, to the idealization of beauty, to the dream of a world perfectly in harmony with art's vision. Which is why it transcends epochs and limits of taste. At this point we must admit that it is impossible to let go of the dream of art as applied to the intrinsic functions of our existence. Beyond time. Beyond culture. Beyond changing fashions. Beyond the chapters of art history. Let us allow ourselves to be overwhelmed, finally, by this mysterious sense of infinity. Mariuccia Casadio

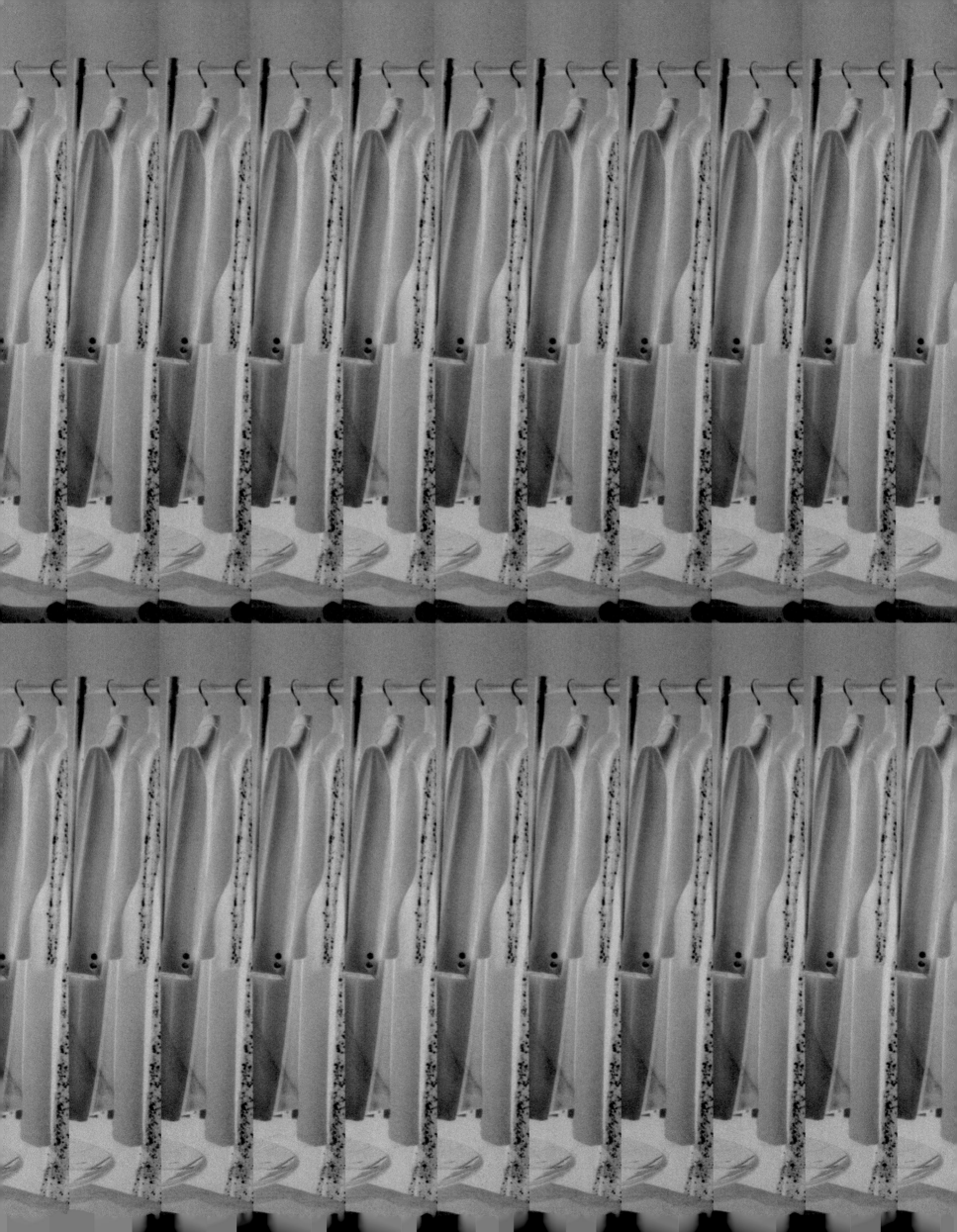

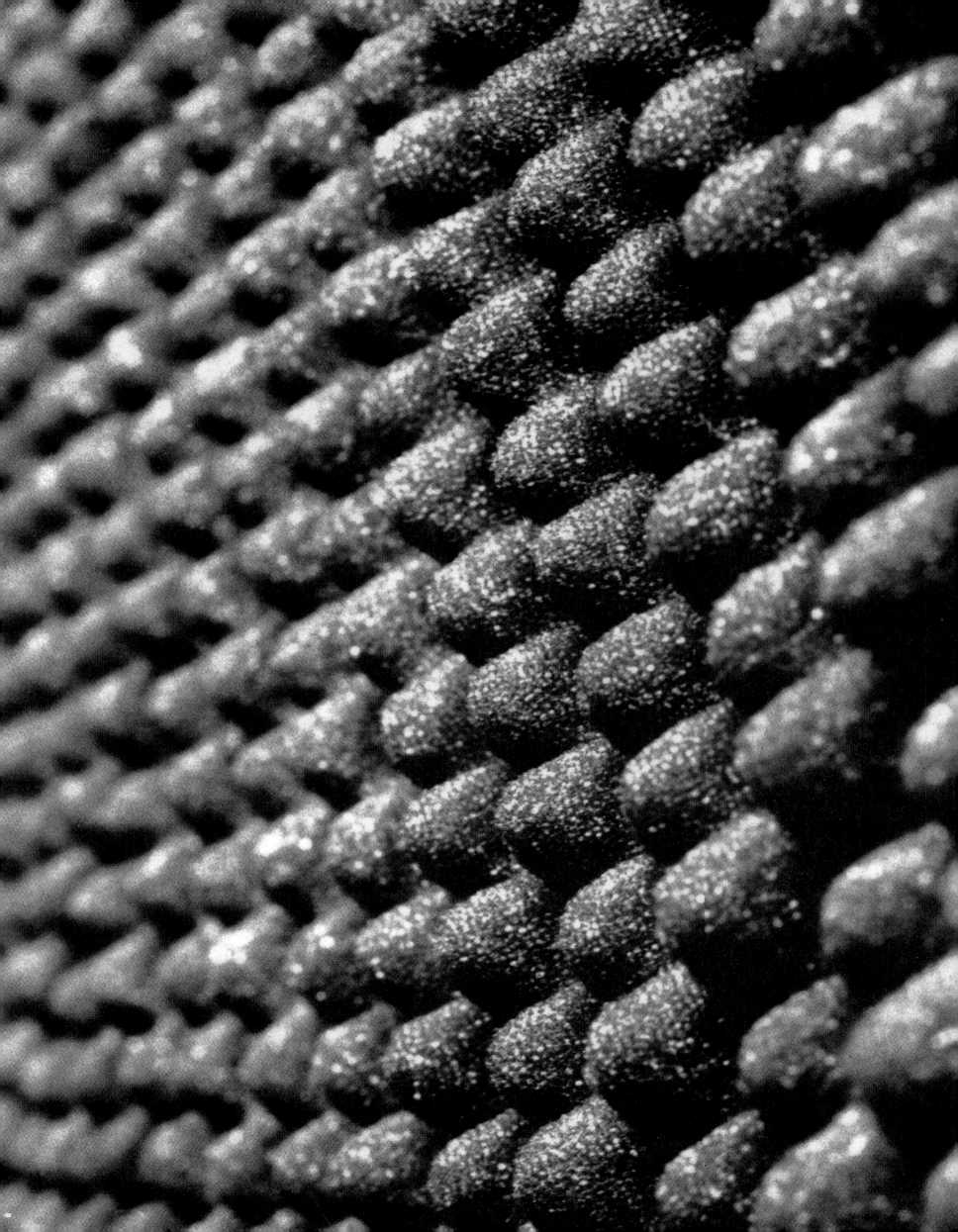

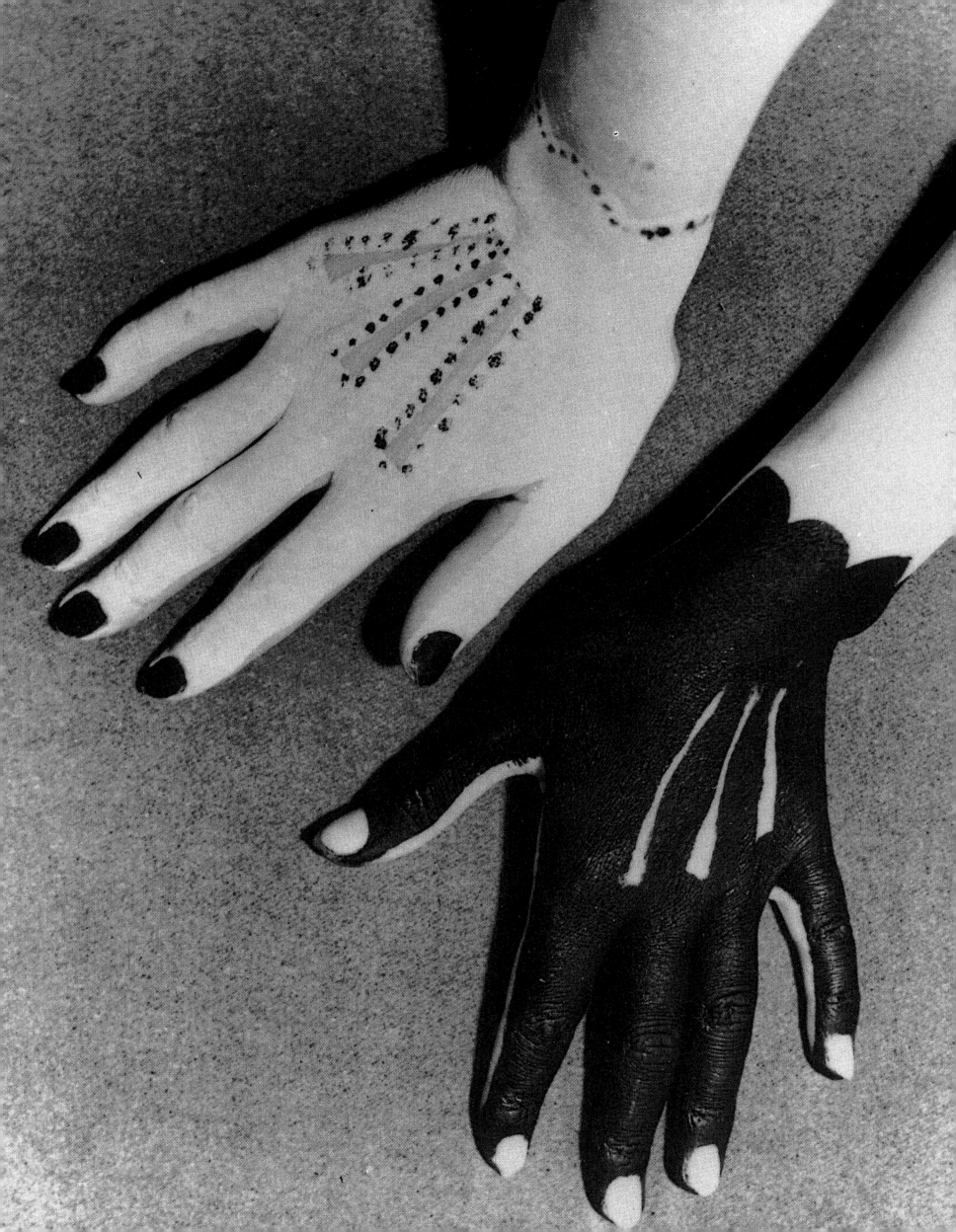

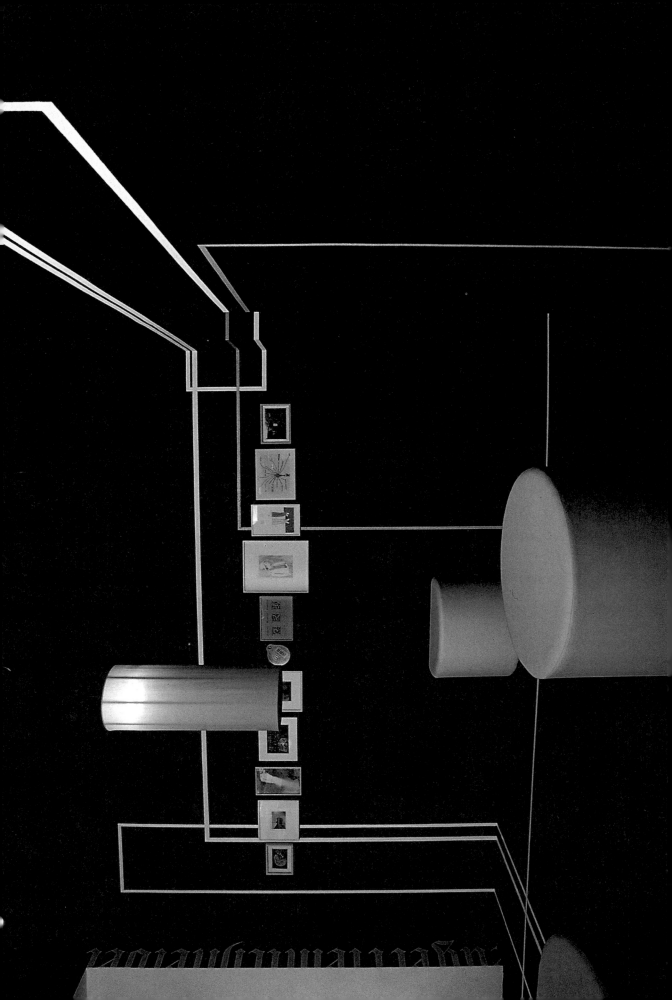

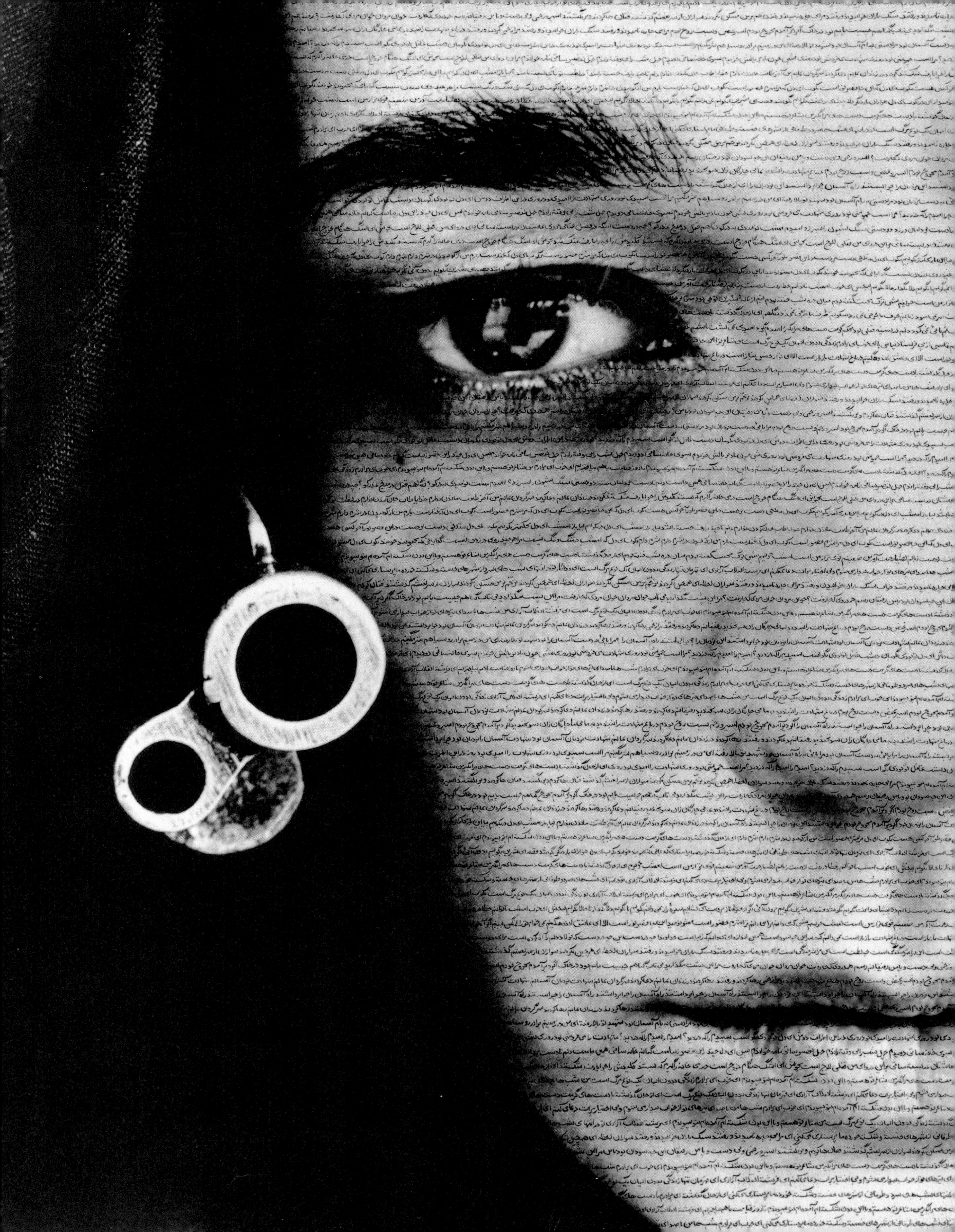

BLACK MEANS AND BLACK-OUTS

BLACK is not a color – the painting teachers said

No BLACKS allowed – the signs used to read

Matisse made a show (1946) titled - BLACK is a colou

Tiger Woods is not BLACK enough, some black guys sai

Why can't he be, just BLACK, the others said

What's this about "CABLINASIAN"? This cocktail of Caucasian, black, Indian and Asia

BLACK is an attitude, not a race, someone else said

And what about BLACK and WHITE being dead, because that's what I've read

It's Korgentinian, Blackanese, Hapa..

Color is a very sensitive matter

Let's have more color, I said, but as a David Hammons work showed, the white art world, still dresses in their funeral fashion

MARLENE DUMAS, 1998

If one could sum up black literature with a single metaphor, it would be to describe it as a net crossing the Atlantic Ocean from one shore to the other. The net would be cast somewhere between Dakar and New York, and along its strands stories, characters and traditions would run to and fro. The United States may give birth to half of African fiction, but even then reference is continually made to the fantastical, wisdom-filled storehouse of ancestral Africa. If Afro-American literature has a specific blackness it is this – barring encounters with firmly westernized authoresses like Terry McMillan who, with her *Waiting to Exhale* has topped the US listings with an all-American tale of thirty to forty-year-olds trying to solve the existential problems common to their generation. Meanwhile, writers who deal with issues of civil rights and post-colonial regimes, or who try to salvage the roots of a culture that has become degenerate through the absorption of Western values, sometimes end up getting the Nobel Prize. Needless to say, amid all the tributes one can hear the small voice of Europe's guilty conscience when confronted with the raised voices of a land to which it needs to make amends for many misdeeds. In 1986 the Nobel Prize for Literature was awarded to Nigerian author Wole Soyinka, an excellent novelist and playwright; in 1992 it was awarded to Derek Walcott, a Caribbean poet (*Omeros*; *The Arkansas Testament*); in 1993 it was awarded to Toni Morrison, nom de plume of Chloe Anthony Wofford, US citizen from the state of Ohio, editor at Random House, and one of the few female writers who points a finger at the male chauvinism inherent in Afro-American culture. She has not only celebrated this culture in her novels, but has studied the roots of it, managing (in *Song of Solomon*) to weave into a very contemporary novel symbols and characters that are almost shamanic in dimension. 'They're practical people who accept magic as one of life's basic ingredients,' writes 67-year-old Morrison (who has recently published another novel, *Paradise*) of Afro-Americans. The definition also suits writers who are on this side of the ocean. For instance, the Nigerian novelist Ben Okri, who won the Booker Prize in 1991 with *The Famished Road*. This is another plot which gives a mystical dimension to contemporary life; in this case it is the belief in reincarnation. However, in the late nineties there seems to have been less emphasis on Black African or American writers. This is no doubt the result, in part, of political events like the end of apartheid in South Africa. In book shops today, there is a lighter shade of black in vogue. The European public has discovered the other shore of the Mediterranean. They now listen to Raï and the songs of Oum Kalsoum. They read the products of a literary tradition that also believes in the fantastic on a daily basis, a rediscovery, somehow, of roots that went astray in the Middle Ages, at the time of the popularization of *A Thousand and One Nights*. Many North African writers are translated, but two of the most popular are Egyptian Naguib Mahfuz, thanks again to a Nobel Prize (author of *Arabian Nights and Days*); and Moroccan Tahar Ben Jelloun, author of *Sand Child* and *Sacred Night*. This put him immediately into the 'pseudo-European' writer category, which in turn opened the way for him to win the Prix Goncourt. Elisabetta Planca

COMPOSITIONS

NAME _____

_____

_____

MADE IN U.S.A.

freedom
economics
Utopia
JEDER

25 Jahre
Menschenrechte
25 Jahre Folter

We
are
your
favorite
embarrassments

questa **notte** **ho sognato** lungo **la strada**

He is usually a detective, possibly a journalist and very occasionally a doctor. He's not good-looking, but the strong, hard lines of a face marked by cynicism and a past (of which little revealed besides the fact that he has lived life to its utmost) make him very attractive. Irresistible in fact, like Humphrey Bogart, the most legendary of actors in the genre. Film noir's hero s a loner. He has no friends and, at the very most, he may have a devoted secretary as accomplice. If he has ever been in love, he has lost the woman in question in some obscure past tragedy, so all he is allowed is a bit of guilt-ridden and risky love-making with a friend's wife. As money and appearance mean nothing to him, he is a bit rumpled and almost invariably wears a mac as well as a lit cigarette stuck to his lower lip. The thriller would lose one of its key features in today's furious anti-smoking campaigns. Our hero of the hour is diffident and a man of the world. He has no faith in his dealings with people and no hope in the future despite having dedicated himself to a level of honesty that borders on moral crusading. However he reveals astounding naïveté when he meets his heroine, the classic 'dark lady'. Preferably blond and elegant, she appears at the beginning as the very picture of innocence, the sorry victim of a conspiracy or mystery that she ably makes even more mysterious. Despite the alarming signals that should have put him on his guard, our hero falls straight into her nets. The dark lady has a very particular line in seduction, not at all aimed at conquering the man himself. Whether innocent or guilty, the lady in the thriller is motivated by a desire for liberty wealth and independence and she uses men to get what she is after, weaving a sentimental trap. At the heart of both celluloid and literary detective stories – the two are inseparable – are a crime, a criminal to be revealed and a mystery to unravel, but that is not all there is to them. First of all, we have to consider the term used to describe the genre. Film noir was first used by French critics in 1946 when, as they watched the American films they had been unable to see during the war, they realized that a vein of pessimism, moroseness and cynicism had infiltrated US cinema, especially in the thriller genre. The urban ambience, lit or often unlit streets with crime and corruption lurking around every corner – these mirrored the general distress of humanity. Most critics would point to John Huston's *The Maltese Falcon* (1942) as the beginning of film noir in the US. This film was taken from Dashiell Hammett's eponymous novel, with Humphrey Bogart in the role of the detective Sam Spade. The most rigorous critics consider the thriller genre to have ended with Orson Welles' *Touch of Evil* (1958), who himself took the role of the corrupt American up against honest Charlton Heston who was trying to find out the truth about crimes linked to the drug trade. Films on which everyone agrees include *The Big Sleep*, by Howard Hawks, taken from a Raymond Chandler novel, with Humphrey Bogart and Lauren Bacall, a well-known thriller team, in the leading roles. Another well known team was Alan Ladd and Veronica Lake. Together in real life, Bogart and Bacall also played together in *Dark Passage*, a story about using plastic surgery to wipe out the past, taken from the novel by the classic thriller writer David Goodies. In *The Big Sleep* Bogart is in the role of Philip Marlowe, the private detective to whom many actors have lent their faces, including Dick Powell and Robert Mitchum. Some other well-known films are: *Sunset Boulevard* by Wilder with Gloria Swanson, the most remarkable of the dark ladies; *Asphalt Jungle* again by Huston, taken from Burnett's novel, with Sterling Hayden (and an appearance by Marilyn Monroe); *The Big Knife* by Robert Aldrich with Jack Palance and Ida Lupino; *The Big Heat* by Fritz Lang with Glenn Ford and Gloria Grahame, *Double Indemnity* by Wilder with Fred McMurray, Barbara Stanwyck and Edward G. Robinson, three extraordinary interpreters of thriller movies. *Double Indemnity* was taken from the eponymous novel by James Cain, author of *The Postman Always Rings Twice*. This last movie is a film noir landmark which has appeared on screen a few times: with John Garfield and Lana Turner, with Clara Calamai and Massimo Girotti in Visconti's Italian version, and not least with the Jack Nicholson/Jessica Lange team. But thrillers are not only an American genre. A few well-known faces from French cinema are pure film noir, for instance, Eddie Constantine, Simone Signoret, Jean Gabin not to mention Jeanne Moreau and Fanny Ardent in Truffaut's films. Many critics point to the wars, both the 'hot' war and the Cold War, as the underlying cause of the spread of film noir but the boundaries are so vast and indefinable that any one explanation is too simplistic. It is because of this that every critic has a different theory, and every movie buff has different films on his or her list. Visconti's *The Stranger* with Mastroanni, taken from Camus, might be included. Why not Scorsese's *Mean Streets* or *Blade Runner* or *Alien* or Cronenberg's obsessions? Film noir has a special position within the detective thriller genre: it is not the geometric whodunnit of Agatha Christie, in which, once the murderer(s) have been revealed, every detail is explained in an orgy of rationality. In film noir, a detective story merges with a love story, turning it into a genre of its own, a world in which insecurity the impossibility of creating order, ambiguity and duplicity never disappear. With a strong dose of human greed and of Freud, film noir brings us characters that are very close to home – many critics have branded it 'Neo-realism made in the USA', suggesting that the black is within us, that one only has to delve a little into the layers of the unconscious and our own repressed desires to find our own evil, our own deviance. For this reason it is neither a reassuring nor amusing genre and yet is one that will never lose its popularity. Maria Pia Lara

11 ~~xxx~~ An ugly ~~xxxx~~ *old* man with a blindfold ~~over his weeping~~ *stained and bloody*
right eye watches the stage intently with his good left eye.

12 (xxx) A young woman ~~~~ the stage, peering over the hem of
her uplifted apron ~~~~ ~~~~ on a straight fold under her nose.

13 ~~xxxxx~~ ~~~~ ~~~~ pinching and jabbing at one
another ~~~~ ~~~~ dogs. One of them has ~~~~
blood on the ~~~~

14 ~~xxxx~~ A middle-aged ~~~~ man sitting very upright with folded
arms and a stern ~~~~ ~~~~ vigorously every few minutes as
though he ~~~~ ~~~~ ~~~~ hearing.

15 ~~xxxxx~~ Two old men ~~~~ are forever changing their
ja~~~~ ~~~~ their ~~~~ running one another's
errands ~~~~

16 ~~xxxx~~ A ~~~~ ~~~~ eyelashes blacken ~~
keeps ~~~~ ~~~~ ~~~~ pocketed on the inside
pocket ~~~~ ~~~~ eyebrows with a spittle
wet ~~~~ finger ~~~~

17 ~~xxxx~~ A little face ~~~~ ~~~~ blood into his
handkerchief. His ~~~~ and ~~~~ wife looks on disapprovingly.

18 ~~xxxxx~~ A middle-aged woman keeps shutting her eyes tight so
that she doesn't see anything to disturb her. However, she often opens
her eyes at the wrong moment and squeals at seeing something she
thinks she should ~~~~ ~~~~

19 ~~xxxxx~~ A middle-aged woman keeps counting the ~~~~ le in the
audience as though she was conducting some form of unspecified
head-count for official reasons. She has great problems counting
because of all the movement. She never finishes and has to repeatedly
start again. *of the audience.*

20 ~~xxxxx~~ An elderly man tries to ~~~~ ~~~~ the main dialogue
lines spoken on stage, but in a whisper ~~~~ ~~~~ his three female
relatives; his middle-aged wife, his ~~~~ ~~~~ his young PG 94
daughter ~~~~ unsuccessfully try to si~~~~ ~~~~ their hands over his
mou~~~~ ~~(nevertheless)~~ continue ~~~~

Black is bourgeois Protestant ethics, the colour of the new man who no longer believes in blood, in the beginning, but only in his own constructions. Who speaks to God without intermediaries. It is the colour of the man who will have to live with his doubt as there is no longer anyone to 'absolve' him or 'assure' him of a state of grace. Hamlet is black. Black is evasion, it underlines the absence of grace. It is non-participation in the world, in the colour of the world. It is ever-heightened aestheticism. It is a Narcissistic delirium, the wanting to be sure that one's own essential presence will be noticed. But it is also nostalgia – the desire to conjure the atmosphere of the theatre: before electricity made the stage uniform, actors sprang forth like ghosts from shadow to light, from negative to positive as if they were performing in a huge camera obscura. Blackness is to realize that we inhabit a world where we are all priests of a lost religion, and we are united only by a sort of aesthetic melancholy. Black is a metaphor for birth: from nothing we appear knowing that to nothing we will return, like shadows flitting across the stage of the world. Remembering that we must love everything and fall in love with no one. Walter Le Moli

3 : ARABES / ISRAËL.

voir Fairouz a cavella) voix d'enfant
ouma Yasin   en hébreu

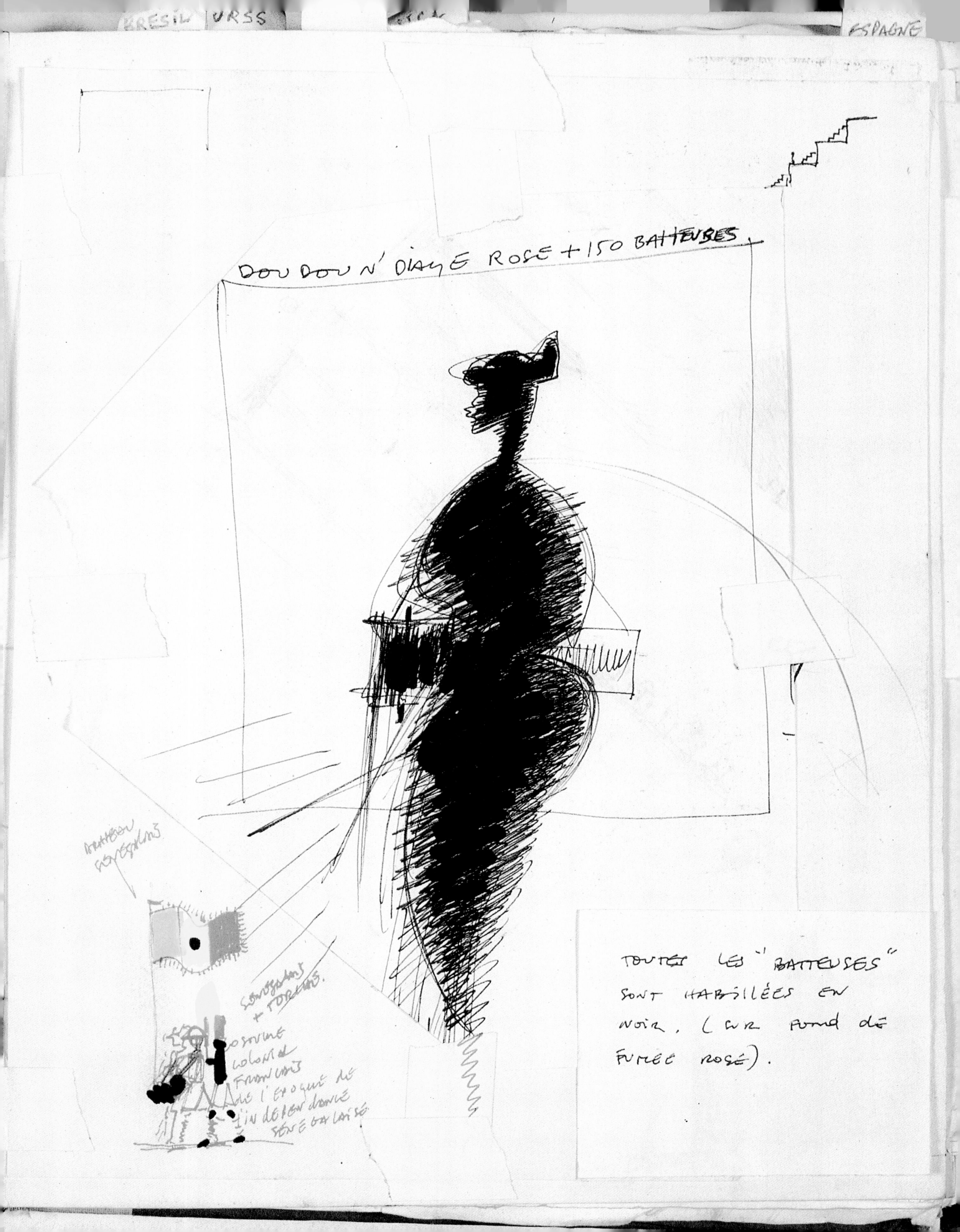

BRESIL
URSS
ESPAGNE
DOUDOU N'DIAYE ROSE + 150 BATTEUSES
DRAPEAU SÉNÉGALAIS
COSTUME COLONIAL FRANÇAIS DE L'ÉPOQUE DE L'INDÉPENDANCE SÉNÉGALAISE
TOUTES LES "BATTEUSES" SONT HABILLÉES EN NOIR. (SUR FOND DE FUMÉE ROSÉ).

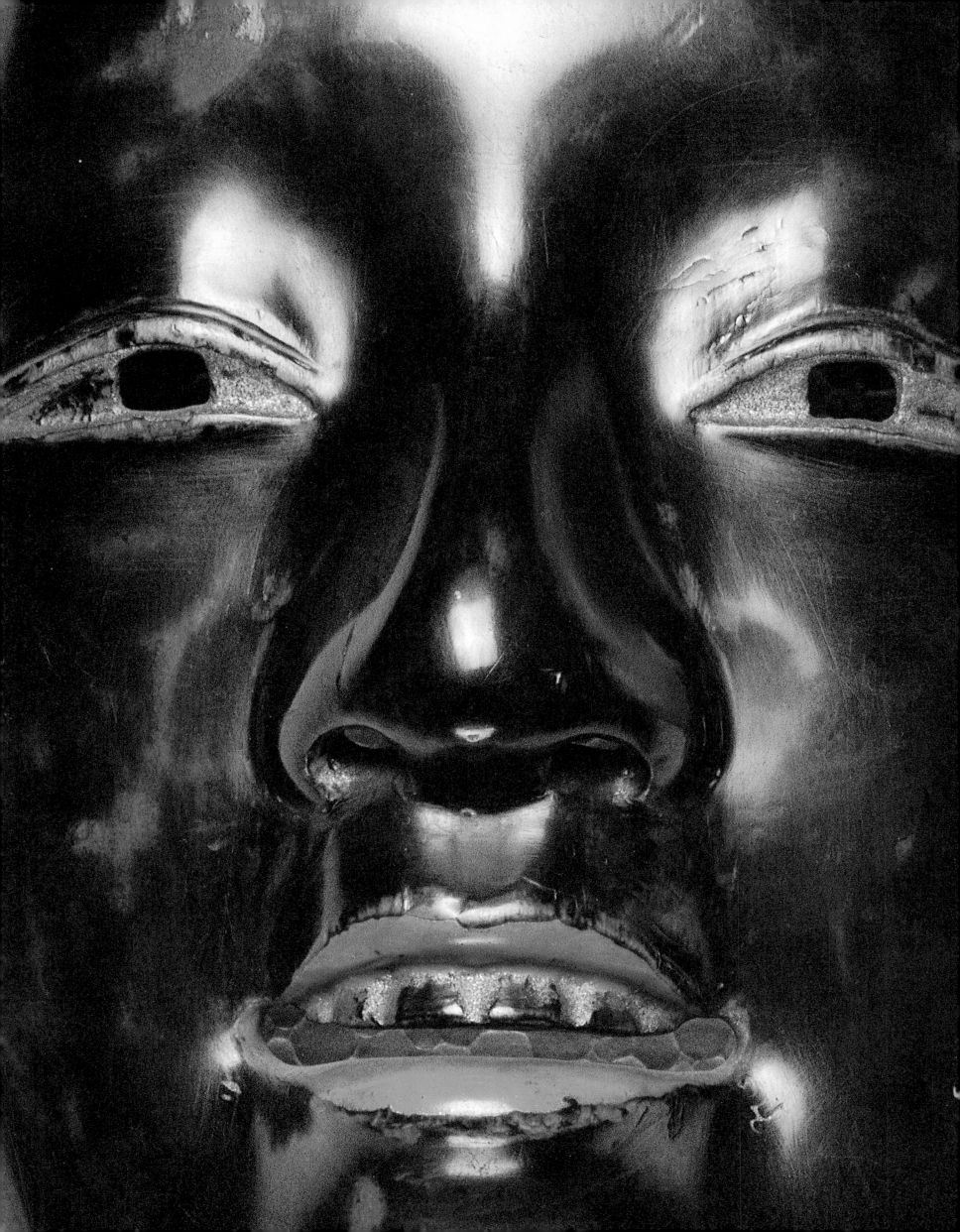

LEFT ON YOUR TEETH

AN OPPOSITION MAN IS CHASED THROUGH
HIS TOWN AND SHOT IN A SMELLING TRAP.
PEOPLE COME TO POKE LIVE FINGERS
THROUGH THE HOLES IN HIM. THEY LOOK
AT THEIR FINGERS TO DIVINE WHETHER
THEY WILL BE SHOT. THEY SHRINK AND
SWELL AND RUN TO HUNT THE PRESIDENT
OF THE NATION WHO SET THE TRAP.

Runaway black. Mysterious river of pitch that cuts a broad swathe across the history of costume and which continues to mark high points in fashion. It is impersonal and magnetic: in a world of paradoxes black has been the colour to robe convention and rebellion, heresy and religion, eroticism and aestheticism, it has united punks and policemen, Hell's Angels and the SS, existentialists and men of society, Hassidic Jews and *femmes fatales*, gothic and Parisian chic, Victorian ladies and rock stars. It is a colour with infinite associations that has imprinted on our memories a whole gallery of characters both from the real world and from the fictional world of cinema and comic strips. It is the leading colour, the passe-partout of contemporary life. The end of this millennium is a good opportunity to sum up the phenomenon of the colour black, spread as it is from royal courts to the latest funky clubs, from nunneries through to iconoclastic fashion parades. It is the colour of immobility and equally the colour of change, as seen in recent years, enhanced by striking a few chords from its richly expressive past – if one takes into account the fact that the black of anti-fashion has always inspired fashion. This black has coloured entire key Spring collections in some cases – an impertinent comment on couture styles, anarchy rearing its head, ambiguous dandyism. A combination of all these elements has taken the season by storm. A designer who has always favoured black to get across an idea, reinforce an image or a creative cut, who is used to thinking out his essential and anti-conventional outfits in black material, Yohji Yamamoto, all in black himself, has a subtle sense of humour and declared punk sympathies. Some time ago he produced a line of evening wear called simply 'Noir'. The Parisian catwalks have paid homage to various shadowy punk and post-punk icons, from Siouxie Sioux, the 'tarantula on stilettos', in fishnets and black leather, to Patti Smith, who could be described as androgynous chaos. Contrast this with the composed silhouettes of the Edwardian age: models dressed entirely in black from the crown of their wide-brimmed hats down to the tips of their gloved fingers. It is a simplified form of what was this century's most lugubrious and incredible display of elegance: Black Ascot, the first races of the season after the death of a king who had put an end to the endless years of Victorian abstinence and given British high society ten unforgettable years of worldly pleasure. It was a sad display of frock coats and top hats, frills and long trains as well as vast picture hats laden with feathers which, according to Cecil Beaton, made the ladies on the lawn look like huge and sinister birds of paradise on their way to some Gothic entertainment. The nation was in mourning not only for the monarch, but also for a world that was disappearing for good, with modernity already jostling into its place. This scene was reproduced in inverted form in the eighties. Inside a hundred-metre circumference around fashion show venues there seemed to stretch an uninterrupted sea of charcoal grey and black. Only this time it featured shabby, squashed headgear pulled down over the eyes along with voluminous patchwork clothing which completely ruled out any notion of anatomy, all worn over ostentatiously spartan shoes. In the royal courtyard of the Louvre, the fashion press, buyers and groupies queued up together to get into the temporary marquees, formed an absurd, surreal vision, calling to mind a witches' coven, according to the more caustic columnists. Western female stereotypes were wiped out by the Black Wave, a cerebral Japanese invention based on asymmetrical superimposition, generated by the same Yohji Yamamoto along with Rei Kawakubo (Comme des Garçons). A new image was created starting from scratch. And starting from black. From a small sect of initiates the message spread, until this fashion avant-garde eventually ceased to exist and was submerged in the wave of street fashion that followed in their wake. Fashion had already been influenced by the subversive black of punk rock some years before, and once again the change in direction was consecrated by an amazing spectacle. At the end of a day at the catwalks, the African club or discotheque 'La Main Bleue', on the outskirts of Paris, saw arrive on its doorstep a veritable flood of four thousand people all dressed in black. The bizarre invitation – '*Moratoire Noire – tenue tragique exigée absolument noire*' (Black Moratorium – totally black tragic dress required) unleashed a veritable frenzy of dressing-up among artists, actors, the fashion world, fashionable world, designers, VIPs, punks and others (including the regular clientele of three hundred black street cleaners), all drawn by the lure of disguises and the opportunity to behave scandalously. A moratorium is a legal act which puts an end to any legal convention. On the evening of the black moratorium it was a case of 'anything goes'. And almost everything happened, right up to the break-in of a real punk gang which led to police intervention and the use of tear gas. To heighten the tension of the drama, in the midst of the vast black space that gave one the impression of drowning, two gymnasts gave an S/M show. Had it not been vetoed by security, there was also going to be a very narrow bridge crossing the void. It was intended as an 'apolitical, asocial, asexual, very liberating' party thrown in honour of Karl Lagerfeld by the young film director Jacques de Bascher. It was a vision of Babylon, a vertiginous plunge into hell, a surrealist delirium, but above all a unique parade of relevant black clothing: from the uniform of an SS officer, worn as a derisive gesture against Nazi fetishes, to the numerous evocations of the expressionist demons of the cinema, amongst which there was a disturbing Golem. The latter was impersonated by Karl Lagerfeld himself, who commented: 'We have had enough of those parties full of blond women with year-round tans, this has been a real novelty.' To be shocking was chic in 1977. To the extent that there were even agencies, like London's 'Rent-a-Punk', which had shock for hire. There is a fatal attraction to a colour that denies itself, and also a mystery factor which cannot be explained away by rational analysis, however interesting this may be. The surges of enthusiasm for black have always aroused interest. John Harvey's *Man in Black* (Reaktion Books, London 1995) tells us how even in the nineteenth century Ruskin, Dickens and Baudelaire wondered why, in a period of extreme wealth and power, men dressed as if they were permanently going to funerals. Dickens even went so far as to compare Queen Victoria's sixty-year reign to a nightmare funeral, with the whole nation in permanent mourning. Women wore black because of the high mortality rates which took away their children and husbands at regular intervals, but more so because of their desire for social distinction which led them to imitate the Queen (who was in perennial widow's weeds after the death of Prince Albert). Apart from black robes, they wore heavy black jet, the *in memoriam* jewellery prescribed by the Court: gloomy bracelets, earrings, châtelaine belt of impressive width – quite effective with the crinoline also in vogue. As far as men were concerned, the new spirit of democracy seems to have made their dress ever more austere and dark. Democracy, according to Baudelaire's original theory, had wiped out individualism and life could no longer be more than 'a mournful procession of dumb-struck bourgeois'. Like death, black was a great leveller. The sombre frock-coat, 'uniform of sorrow', became the symbol of equality. Other critics prefer to find the roots of the ethics of blackness and gloom in Protestantism. It was the values of Protestant countries which became those firstly of nascent capitalism and later on of the industrial society, and then further conditioned our manner of dress. According to the scholar Michel Pastoureau, an expert in the history of social codes, our dark clothing and white shirts, our dinner jackets and evening dress are a more or less direct inheritance from Protestant colour codes which revolved around a triumvirate of black, grey and white. To free ourselves from the tyranny of black, however, we have found a surrogate in navy blue. Even jeans, however faded they may be, were conceived originally as an item of dark clothing, a direct product of Anglo-Saxon Protestant morality. Yet other critics would like to lay the blame entirely on the Catholics, pinpointing the epicentre of the phenomenon in the Spain of the black-robed Inquisition and Philip the Second, the prototype of the sinister and saturnine monarch, who wanted all of his subjects, down to the last man, to dress in black like himself. It is not for nothing that Velázquez immortalized him immersed in a lake of black ink. As in the case of all politically and economically dominant nations, the solemn Spanish black spread to other countries, even contaminating the English Court. Another factor to be considered are the strong links between Spain and the extremely influential Jesuits, an insidious, semi-secret, black-garbed army who were of inspiration to the SS, albeit involuntarily. The deathly Schutz Staffen, elite of the Third Reich, felt black to be the colour of death more than any other group, confirming this belief with menacing skulls attached to their berets. A great admirer of the disciplinary principles upon which the Jesuits were organized, the head of the SS, Himmler, was seen by Hitler as his very own Ignatius of Loyola. Loyal to the Führer in the same way the Jesuits were to the Pope, the SS were regarded as holy warriors. But the most interesting

detail is that for them black was associated with youth. This connotation has survived the war, as can be seen in the revivalist mania of the gangs of bad boys in black – Bikers, Rockers, Hell's Angels, Blousons Noirs, from Wild Man Marlon Brando onwards – for covering themselves in Nazi symbols, swastikas and skulls. Symbols that were turned into sadist fantasies or anarchism and Dada, depending on whether or not you were a punk rocker. From the forties onwards the myth of the outlaw biker has assumed epidemic proportions and the black leather jacket, which has even been adopted by the police force, especially in the United States, has become a universal fetish. It is a curiously ambivalent symbol, the black leather jacket, representing as it does both law-breakers and law-enforcers. It is the chosen uniform of any and every rebel without a cause, from James Dean to the Rockers who, like the idolized American Neurotic Boy, enjoyed heading for unknown destinations with a foot hard down on the accelerator, poised on a knife-edge between extreme speed and death. Although the simple, black, roll-necked jumper with trousers or skirt of the social-convention defying bohemian does not have the same romantic aura of danger, it is no less revealing. The standard wear of existentialists, beatniks, artists and students, the black that acclaims the importance of thought, of intellectual power, is as alive and vital today as it ever was. It is underwritten by famous names and venues, from the smoke-filled jazz clubs of Saint Germain-des-Prés to Juliette Gréco, from hard bop poetry to the beat generation of Ginsberg, Kerouac, Burroughs, Corso and Ferlinghetti, and is destined to increase its fascination, now a reminder of a period that has become a new mythology for us. At the other end of the scale we have the 'petit rien noir', the unbeatable 'thrown-together' evening dress launched by Chanel in the twenties and cultivated also by Givenchy, which received its screen début in the early sixties with Audrey Hepburn. Among the great masters of black it would be impossible not to mention Balenciaga, who managed to give the colour the additional aura of a peculiarly Spanish dramatic depth, whilst Saint Laurent has been successful in our time in playing the card of provocative sensuality, with his historic nude-look of 1968, street fashion derived from bikers, beatniks and existentialists, and formalism expressed in his admirable dinner jackets. It has to be pointed out, with regards to the latter, that black, the leading colour of androgynous fashion, has always put a subtle emphasis on the diabolic, from Marlene Dietrich in her top hat and tails to Madonna with her masculine get-ups and monocle. Black pervades every aspect of contemporary life. It is found in the pages of the magazines of youth culture and in the rock music scene. It is perpetuated by the dark figure of Robert Smith of the Cure, who immortalized the Gothic look in the early eighties, and by a whole series of recent cult movies, including David Lynch's *Lost Highway*, *Gattaca* with Uma Thurmann, Jan Kounen's *Doberman*, Wim Wender's *The End of Violence*, *Blues Brother's 2000* by John Landis and *Black Out* by Abel Ferrara, not to mention the deep Sicilian black brought into contemporary fashion by Dolce & Gabbana. One thing is certain: beyond all the possible meanings we may want to give to the colour black, it will remain the perfect ally of anyone at all, so long as they are significant. In itself it contains all colour, intensity and light. Lele Acquarone

Black Music. Only a decade ago this could have been a label for a very clearly defined sound. Today, in the era of the global village and ever fairer-skinned Michael Jacksons, it no

longer conveys the same meaning. In the eighties and nineties black music has made gradual but irreversible inroads into pop and rock music, which by tradition were white and

WASP arenas. This has earned black musicians great popular credibility in their own departments: rap, reggae and soul. Black, in other words, is in and getting bigger. It is fashionable

(the frontiers of rap have lately been spilling over into acid jazz), intellectual (look at the involvement of singer-songwriters like Ben Harper or Tracy Chapman), gets into the blood

(as in ethnic African rhythms) and is danceable (e.g. Whitney Houston's mellow soul) all at once. To obtain these results, mass recognition and appreciation at an international level,

has not been easy. Neither has it been painless. Only fifty years ago white America contemptuously called the blues and gospel sung by black singers or groups 'race music'. However,

at the same time they were already hooked on Louis Armstrong, Count Basie and Charlie Parker's jazz. At the end of the Second World War, things changed: 'white' radio stations

started to broadcast 'black' music, coloured musicians were to be seen more and more often in fashionable music venues and the recording industry realized the potential of black

musicians. They swamped the market with 45s and LP vinyl cut by energetic blues singers (Muddy Waters, B.B. King), crooners and ballad singers (Nat King Cole, The Platters), hip

funk dancers (James Brown), and gospel singers (Ray Charles, Dinah Washington). The elevation of black music to the highest heights starts here, prior to and alongside the explosion

of rock and roll. From this moment onwards it became more and more difficult to do without black rhythms, even for white musicians. The first rock-and-roll sounds to come out in

the fifties came from black musicians – from Chuck Berry to Little Richard and from Bo Diddley to Fats Domino – and this comes as no surprise. Neither does it come as a surprise

that the enterprise boasting about being the most successful firm with 'coloured' capital in the United States in the sixties was a recording company, Motown, with many famous

names on its labels: the Jackson Five, the Temptations, Stevie Wonder, the Supremes, Marvin Gaye and the Four Tops. It is almost superfluous to recall that in the same decade, it

was a non-white guitarist, Jimi Hendrix, who taught his white fellow-musicians about technique and feeling. Isolated cases? On the contrary: this pattern is continued in the seventies

with the explosion of Bob Marley's reggae and disco music from Sylvester, Chic and Donna Summer, not to mention the official entry into Hollywood film scores of black music, with

leading figures such as Isaac Hayes, Curtis Mayfield, James Brown and Diana Ross. This sealed the non-coloured public's acceptance of black music. However, the real crossover,

the full marriage of black rhythms and rock guitar, of pop tunes and soul danceability, took place in the following decade. Thanks to big names like Michael Jackson and Prince,

the frontiers between white rock and black music became more and more blurred, in the same way as the skin colour of the musician lost any definite connotations. It was rap,

however, that balanced the scales, dealing solely with street (black) issues with totally black urban rhythms. But even this could not slow down the unstoppable race towards

universal affirmation: to the point of bringing about the birth of white rap groups who sing their verses loud and clear at the most acclaimed black rappers. Paolo Scarpellini

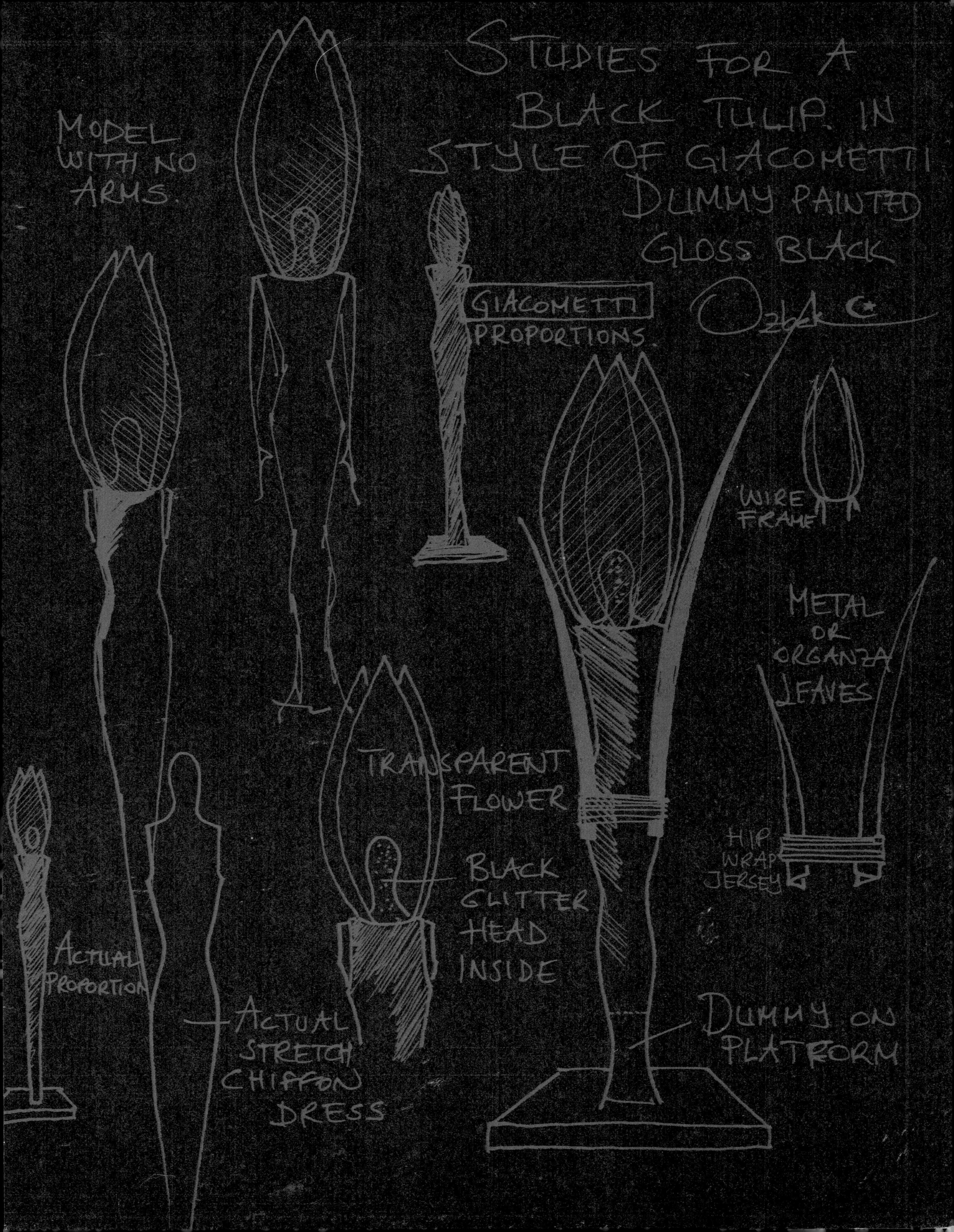

MODEL WITH NO ARMS.

STUDIES FOR A BLACK TULIP. IN STYLE OF GIACOMETTI DUMMY PAINTED GLOSS BLACK

Ozbek ☾

GIACOMETTI PROPORTIONS.

WIRE FRAME

METAL OR ORGANZA LEAVES

ACTUAL PROPORTION

TRANSPARENT FLOWER

BLACK GLITTER HEAD INSIDE

HIP WRAP JERSEY

ACTUAL STRETCH CHIFFON DRESS

DUMMY ON PLATFORM

In photography, black is half of the work. By definition, without it, there would be nothing left of the film but a white expanse of burnt camera exposure. Photography exists through the balancing of opposites. Among art forms it is possibly the one that best demonstrates how light is actually born, from dark. Few images can evoke luminosity and brilliance better than the deep, velvety black of certain night shots taken by Mario Giacomelli; or the extraordinary work of Antonio Biasiucci in which we see folds of corrugated lava from the Vesuvius or the hide of a cow transformed into a dark expanse – where only in a corner do you catch the glint of the animal's open eye. In the work of these and other Italian photographers (from Biasiucci to Enzo Sellerio, the photographer of Sicilian scenes, from Marianna Capelli to Maurizio Buscarino, critic and actor in the nihilist plays of Kantor), the black of black-and-white appears more as a state of the spirit than a means of expression. It permeates the images, and steeps them in the light of obscurity. However, the colour black in photography has a physical dimension, more than a metaphysical one. It has given a voice to the world of black humanity, to the African peoples. From the mid-1800s onwards, this white people's art form found itself confronted with the naturally photogenic bodies and faces of dark-skinned peoples. The photographic history of blacks unfolds, at least until the end of the forties, in front of the lens and not behind it. In the latter half of last century, with the colonial era in full swing, French, Italian and German documentary makers opened up shop in the capital cities of Morocco, Egypt and Mali and produced images half-way between folklore and ethnography. These were then purchased by civil servants stationed out there, to be brought back as trophies of the exoticism of those far-away lands. With the excuse of anthropological study, female nudes were quite legitimate, which provided an extreme challenge to the all-pervading prudery of that era, and contributed to the later association, in the European mind, of the black and Eros. The black then became both the subject of the camera lens and an object of desire. Aware of the power of their allure in the eyes of the white man who observed them, the subjects allowed their portraits to convey a tacit implication of sexuality. Given that the observer was normally male, as well as white, this resulted in the creation of a whole paradigm of homosexual beauty. This is implicit in the passive and

ironically languid young Tunisians posing for the author of *Under the Sheltering Sky*, Paul Bowles (the publisher Scalo of Zurich dedicated a handsome book recently to Paul Bowles' photography). It is explicit to the point of obscenity in Robert Mapplethorpe's models. He gets the best out of the turgid and velvety texture of the testes, members and naked bodies thanks to his perfect printing techniques and the play of light and fluids between black skin and other surfaces. Even a chaste portrait like *Djimon with Octopus* takes on powerful erotic undertones. In fact, Western imagination has so imbued the black male body with sexual value that even the ironic nudes invented by Charlotte March in the seventies are perturbing (invented for *twen* and for the photographic book *Man, Oh! Man*). This is an aspect that disappears when it is blacks that photograph blacks, but we have to wait until the fifties for this. In New York Roy De Carava, an employee in a printing works, kills the boredom of his daily routine by taking photos of the blacks who, like him, take the subway every morning to go to work. When he becomes a professional photographer (in 1947), he falls in love with Coltrane's saxophone and produces a series of smoky, atmospheric portraits of the musician that go down in jazz and photographic history. In the same years Gordon Parks was working on his images of Harlem. With Emerging Man, the face of a black man of which only half comes to the surface of the photo, he pays an implicit tribute to the novels of Ralph Ellison, author of *The Invisible Man*. On the other side of the ocean, in sub-Saharan Africa, in the wake of the French photographers from the colonial era, a tradition of native photography is in its infancy. From the late forties to the sixties, young Senegalese and Malians went to the Mama Casset Studios in Dakar and to Seydou Keita in Bamako to get their portraits done. They were decked out in a range of clothing and accessories: women, whose hair was plaited with brightly-coloured wool, wearing gold ornaments and flowery calicos, the men dressed in European-style dandy zoot suits, illustrating, apart from the quality of the photography, the westernization of the two countries. A notable aspect is the surprising nonchalance of the models, whether young or not-so-young, elegant girls or *griots* – traditional bards – as they pose before an always suspect device, witchcraft capable of stealing the *dyaa*, the soul of whoever stands before it. Elisabetta Planca

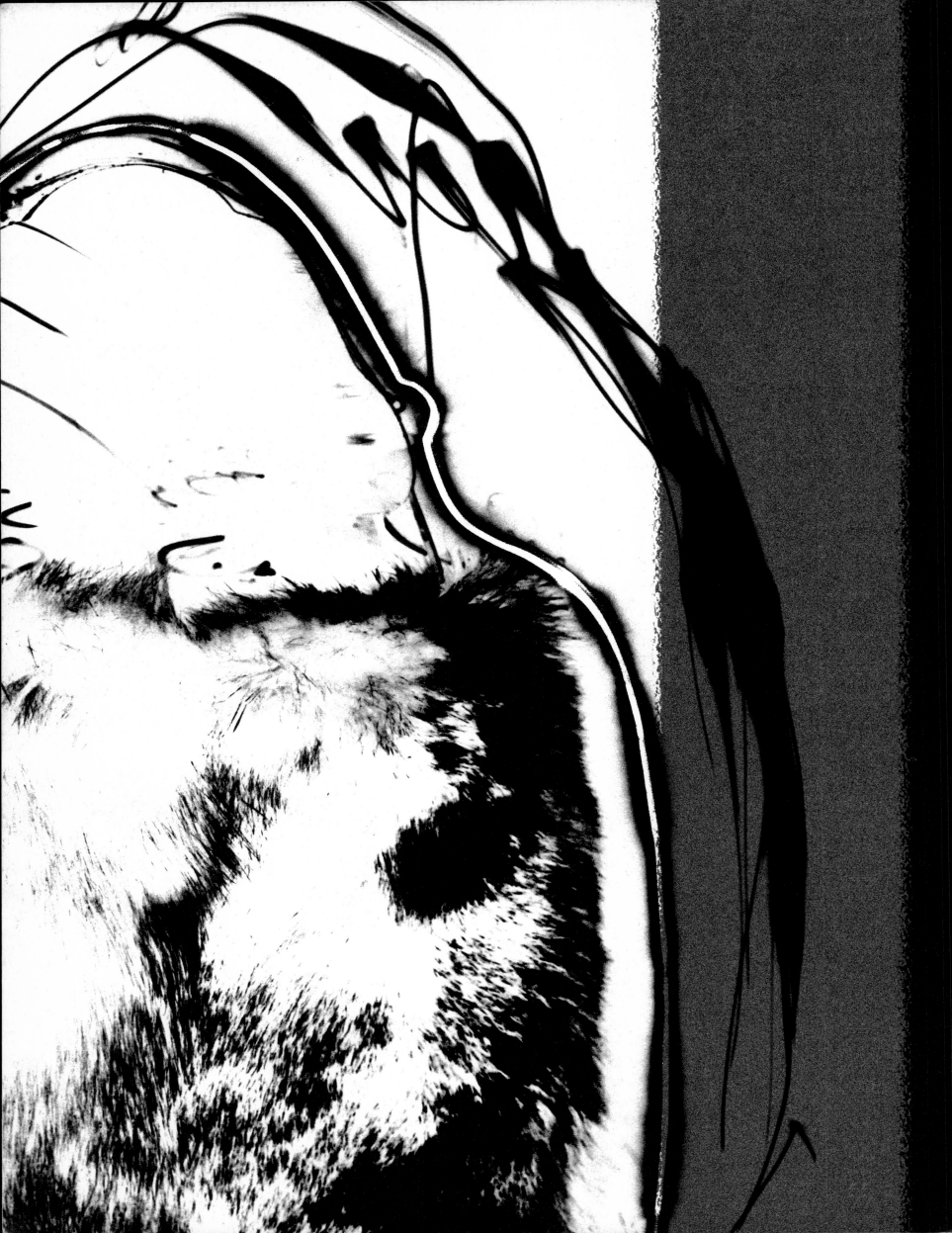

p. 6 Damien Hirst, *Untitled Black Monochrome (Without Emotion) – Landscape*, 1997. Courtesy of Prada Foundation, Milan.

pp. 16–17 Jannis Kounellis, *Untitled*, 1965. Private collection Frankfurt-am-Main. © Jannis Kounellis.

p. 18 Gennaro Avallone, *Impression*, 1998. Screen.

pp. 20–21 Bruce Weber. Collage of 80 photos.

pp. 20–23 Bruce Weber. Portraits of Nelson Mandela.

p. 24 Marlene Dumas, *Michael Jackson as Jesus*, 1994. G. Testa Collection, Milan. Courtesy of Le Case d'Arte, Milan.

p. 25 Marlene Dumas, *Joséphine*, 1997. A. Grassi Collection, Milan. Courtesy of Le Case d'Arte, Milan.

p. 26 Benedict Fernandez, *Protest: Hassidic Group*, 1978. © Benedict J. Fernandez of Almanac.

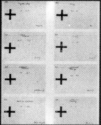

p. 27 Enzo Sellerio, *Sanfratello (Messina), Good Friday procession*, 1962. © Enzo Sellerio.

p. 28 Jean-Paul Gaultier, photo Deborah Turbeville. Paris 1998.

p. 29 Joseph Beuys, *Untitled*, 1968. Private collection, Naples. © ADAGP, 1998.

p. 30 Ludwig Mies van der Rohe/Sergius Ruegenberg, floor of Barcelona pavilion, 1929.

p. 31 Punk Movement. Photo Degen Thomas, in *Body Painting*. © Frederking & Thaler, Munich, 1994.

p. 32 Kasimir Malevich, book cover *From Cubism and Futurism to Suprematism*, third edition, Moscow 1916.

p. 33 Richard Serra, *Terminal*, work for Documenta VI, Kassel 1977. © ADAGP, 1998. Photo Dieter Schwille, Cologne.

p. 34 Julian Schnabel, *Virtue*. 1986.

p. 35 Robert Mapplethorpe, *Black X*, 1983. © The Estate of Robert Mapplethorpe. Used by permission.

p. 36 Kcho, *Estelas en la mar mi abrigo y my sosten [Wakes in the sea my shelter and support] (Mariana)*, 1996. Courtesy of Guenzani Studio, Milan.

p. 37 James Van Der Zee, *Black Cross Nurses*, 1924. © Donna Van Der Zee.

p. 38 Ezaki Reiji, *Five men*, ca. 1880. © Berliner Festspiele, Argon Verlag.

p. 39 Man Ray, *Study of Hands*, 1928. © Man Ray Trust/ADAGP, 1998.

p. 40 Comme des Garçons, photo by Paolo Roversi. Tokyo 1998.

p. 41 Comme des Garçons, photo by Paolo Roversi. Tokyo 1998.

p. 42 John Galliano for Dior, photo by Paolo Roversi. Paris 1998.

p. 43 Mario Merz, *Painter in Africa*, 1984. Castello di Rivoli, Turin.

p. 44 Dolce & Gabbana, photo Giovanni Gastel. Milan 1998.

p. 45 Ivan Seviakov, covering of icon *Mother of God of Theodorus*, Kostroma, 1792

p. 46 Christian Lacroix, Christian Lacroix design. Paris 1998.

p. 47 Giambattista Tiepolo, *Woman with a Tricorn Hat*, ca. 1755–60. Samuel Kress Collection. © Board of Trustees, National Gallery of Art, Washington, 1998.

p. 48 Victor Burgin, *Portia*, private collection, 1984.

p 49 Anish Kapoor, *Descent into Limbo*, 1992. Project for Documenta IX, Kassel, 1992. © Anish Kapoor, Ed. Charta, Milan.

pp. 50–51 Bruce Weber. Portrait of Louise Bourgeois. New York 1997.

p. 52 Tom Dixon, *Jack*, 1997.

p. 53 Andreas Schulze, *Untitled*, 1983, private collection. Courtesy of Monika Sprüth Gallery, Cologne.

p. 54 Nigel Coates, *Legover Chair*, 1997.

p. 55 Giorgio Armani, photo by Maria Vittoria Backhaus. Milan 1998.

p. 56 Carlo Mollino, design, ca. 1965. From *Carlo Mollino*, Idea Books Editions, 1985, Milan. © Idea Books.

p. 57 Robert Morris, *Untitled*, 1973. Courtesy of Philomene Magers Gallery, Cologne, and Sonnabend Gallery, New York.

p. 59 Walter Dahn, *Copyright Man*, 1986. Emilio Haiman Collection. Courtesy of Le Case d'Arte, Milan.

p.60 Eleanore Mikus, *Tablet 152*, 1966. From *Eleanore Mikus – Shadows of the Real*, Groton House, Ithaca, New York. © Eleanore Mikus, 1991. Photo: Lee Helen. Northlight.

pp. 62–63 Keith Haring, *Happy Boys*, 1989. © Estate of Keith Haring. Consolandi Collection Milan.

p. 64 Thierry Mugler, Mats Gustafson design. Paris 1998.

p. 65 Pino Pascali, *Shark Fins*, 1967. © Faggionato Fine Arts London.

p. 66 Prada, photo by Peter Lindbergh. Milan 1998.

p. 67 Donna Karan, photo by Oberto Gili. New York 1998.

p. 68 Rolf Sachs, *Ha-all*, 1994.

p. 69 Denis Santachiara, thermal scooter jacket, 1998.

p. 70 Alighiero Boetti, *Twins*, 1968. Courtesy Alighiero Boetti Archives, Rome.

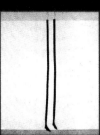

p. 71 Louise Bourgeois, *Legs*, 1986. Private collection. © Louise Bourgeois. Photo by Robert MacDonald.

p. 72 Bruna Bini and Lucio Fontana dress, 1961, Bini Collection. Photo by Maria Vittoria Backhaus.

p.73 Ugo Mulas, portrait of Lucio Fontana, Milan, 1965. © Ugo Mulas Archives, Milan.

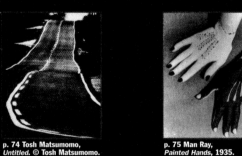

p. 74 Tosh Matsumomo, *Untitled*. © Tosh Matsumomo.

p. 75 Man Ray, *Painted Hands*, 1935. © Man Ray Trust/ADAGP, 1998.

p. 76 Robert Longo, *Untitled*, 1983. A. Grassi Collection, Milan. Courtesy of Metro Pictures, New York.

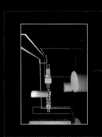

p. 77 Vassily Kandinsky, *Gnomus*, ca. 1928. Theatre Museum of Cologne University. © ADAGP, 1998.

p.79 Peter Fischli & David Weiss, *Moroccan Cushion*, 1987. Rossi Collection, Turin. Courtesy of Le Case d'Arte, Milan.

p. 80 Portrait of a young girl, Rashaïda. © Fabby Nielsen.

p. 81 Katharina Fritsch, *Tischgesellschaft*, 1988, private collection. Courtesy of the Museum of Modern Art, Frankfurt-am-Main.

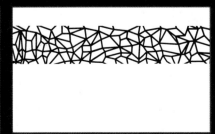

pp. 82–83 Sol Lewitt, *Wall Drawing*, 1989. Photo by Salvatore Licitra. Courtesy of Le Case d'Arte, Milan.

p. 84 From *L'Art calligraphique de l'Islam*, Editions Gallimard, 1994. © Mohamed Sijelmassi.

p. 78 Tobias Rehberger, view of Brancusi installation, 1997. Courtesy of Neugerriemschneider Gallery, Berlin.

p. 85 Raghubir Singh. Photo of Hindu Believer, (Gröning Archives). From *Body Painting*. © Frederking & Thaler, Munich, 1994.

p. 86 Azzedine Alaïa,
photo Peter Lindbergh.
Paris 1998.

p. 87 Shirin Neshat,
Speechless, 1996.
Courtesy of Marco Noire,
Turin.

p. 90 Cy Twombly, *Untitled*,
1967. Courtesy of Karsten
Greve Gallery, Cologne, Paris,
Milan.

p. 91 Roy Lichtenstein,
Composition I, 1964.
Courtesy of Modern Art
Museum, Frankfurt-am-Main.
© Roy Lichtenstein,
New York/ADAGP, 1998.

p. 92 Joseph Beuys, (a)
Museum of Modern Art,
Oxford, (b) *Directional Forces*,
ICA, London 1974. © The
Solomon R. Guggenheim
Foundation, 1979. Photo Ute
Klophaus. © Caroline Tisdall.

p. 93 James Van Der Zee,
portrait of Jean Michel
Basquiat, 1982.
© Donna Van Der Zee.

p. 94 Barbara Kruger,
Untitled, 1985. A. Grassi
Collection. Courtesy of Le
Case d'Arte, Milan.

p. 95 Gilles Caron, *Rue Saint-
Jacques, 6th May 1968.
Paris*. © Gilles Caron/Contact
Press Images/Grazia Neri.

p. 96 Andy Warhol, *Most
Wanted Man No. 3, Ellis Ruez
B.*, 1964; *Most Wanted Man
No. 4. Redmond C.*, 1964;
*Most Wanted Man No. 5,
Arthur Alvin M.*, 1964.
© ADAGP, 1998.

p. 97 Piero Manzoni,
Identity Check, 1961.
© ADAGP, 1998.

p. 98 Rosemarie Trockel, *Lisa*,
1993. Courtesy of Monika
Sprüth Gallery, Cologne.

p. 99 Alberto Burri,
Black Plastic 1, 1962.
Courtesy of Palazzo Albizzini
Foundation, Perugia.

p. 100 Botto e Bruno,
*Last Night I Dreamt Along
the Road*, 1998.

p. 101 Calvin Klein,
New York 1998.

p. 102 Gabriel Orozco,
Stone that Gives Way, 1992.
Courtesy of Monica de
Cardenas.

p. 103 Fabrizio Ferri,
Black Pearls, Tahiti 1990.

p. 104 Versace, photo by
Maria Vittoria Backhaus.
Milan 1998.

p. 105 Anselm Kiefer,
from *Ausbrenne des
Landkreises Buken VII*, 1975.
© Abbildungen Anselm Kiefer.
Photo Uwe H. Seyl,
John Abbot.

p. 106 Brad Lewis.
Lava Flow.
© Brad Lewis/Age/Cosmos.

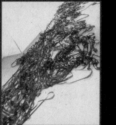
p. 107 Ivo Bonacorsi,
1km of Photographic Film,
1996. Photo Giovanni Ricci.
Courtesy of Bordone Gallery,
Milan.

p. 108 Krizia.
Photo Paolo Roversi.
Milan 1998.

p. 109 Eva Marisaldi,
Suggestion, 1995.
Photo by Lucio Costa.

p. 111 Peter Greenaway,
Head Text Series – A, 1994.
Courtesy of Nicole
Klagesbourg, New York.

p. 112 Vincenzo Castella,
*Sleepy John Estes,
Brownsville, Tn. (USA)*, 1976.
Courtesy Le Case d'Arte,
Milan.

p. 113 Michelangelo
Pistoletto, film still from
L'Homme noir by Pierre
Coulibeuf, 1997.

p. 114 Pier Paolo Pasolini
and Anna Magnani, 1962.
Courtesy of Fratelli Fabbri
Editori and Incontri
Internazionali d'Arte, Rome.

p. 116 Bruce Weber.
Portrait of Patti Smith.

p. 117 Martha Graham.
© Dance collection/New York
Public Library.

p. 118 Jean-Paul Goude.
Design.

p. 119 Jean-Paul Goude.
Design.

p. 120 Nô theatre mask.
© Priuli & Verlucca Editori
and Geneva Museum of
Ethnography. Photo Attilio
Boccazzi – Varotto.

p. 121 Jenny Holzer,
Under a Rock, 1986.
A. Grassi Collection, Milan.
Courtesy of Monika Sprüth,
Cologne.

p. 123 Sylvie Fleury,
New Season, 1997.
View of installation.
Courtesy of Philomene
Magers Gallery, Cologne.

p. 125 Alexander McQueen,
photo by Paolo Roversi.
London 1998.

p. 126 Frank Stella,
Turkish Mambo, 1959.
Courtesy of Christie's
New York.

p. 127 Helmut Newton.
Men's suit, Yves Saint Laurent.
1971.

p. 128 Karl Lagerfeld. Black dress, Karl Lagerfeld. Paris 1998.

p. 129 Alaister Thain. Gilbert & George. © Alaister Thain.

pp. 130–131 Peter Lindbergh. Photos from *Vogue* Italy, September 1997.

p.132 Robert Mapplethorpe, Lisa Lyson, 1981. © The Estate of Robert Mapplethorpe. Used by permission.

p. 133 Rosemarie Trockel, *Untitled*, 1991. Courtesy of Monika Sprüth Gallery, Cologne.

p. 134 Karen Kilimnik, *Gia, Cindy, Bubble Gum Habit*, 1993. Courtesy of Il Capricornio Gallery, Venice.

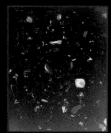
p. 135 Sue Williams, *Foot with Choices*, 1996. Courtesy of Il Capricornio Gallery, Venice.

pp. 136–137 Annette Messager, *Mes Voeux*, 1994. Private collection. Courtesy of Monika Sprüth Gallery, Cologne.

p. 138 Robert Mapplethorpe, Lisa Lyson, 1982. © The Estate of Robert Mapplethorpe. Used by permission.

p. 139 Rebecca Horn, film still from *The Widow from Paradise*, 1975. © Cologne Art Museum and Rebecca Horn.

p. 140 Steven Meisel. Portrait of Grace Coddington. *Vogue* Italy.

p. 141 Bruce Weber, from book *Gentle Giants*, 1996.

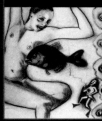
p. 142 Francesco Clemente, *Untitled*, 1989. Modern Art Museum, Frankfurt-am-Main.

p. 144 Zoe Leonard, *Untitled*, 1988/93. Courtesy of Paula Cooper Gallery, New York.

p. 145 Ozbek. *Black Tulip*, London 1998.

p. 146 Andy Warhol, *S.A.S. Passenger Ticket*, 1968. ©ADAGP, 1998.

p. 147 Philip Taaffe, *Little Iris*, 1985. A. Grassi Collection, Milan.

p. 148 Enzo Cucchi, Monte Tamaro Chapel, Lugano 1994.

p. 149 Manolo Blahnik. Design. London 1998.

p. 150 Julian Schnabel, *Sidecar*, 1984.

p. 151 Cindy Sherman, *Untitled Film Still*, 1978. Courtesy Metro Pictures, New York.

p. 153 Helmut Lang, photo Craig McDean. New York 1998.

p. 154 Issey Miyake, photo Barry Lategan. Tokyo 1998.

p. 155 Bernd & Hilla Becher, *Schalker Verein, Gelsenkirchen, Ruhr*, 1982. Courtesy of Le Case d'Arte, Milan.

p. 156 André Putnam, Le Lac, Tokyo, 1989.

p. 157 Gianfranco Ferré, photo Maria Vittoria Backhaus. Milan 1998.

p. 158 Antoine Predock, American Heritage Center, Laramie, Wyoming, 1987–93. © Antoine Predock. Photo Timothy Hursley.

p. 159 Black Pearl from Tahiti. Photo Studio Azzurro.

p. 160 Philip Treacy, photo Nick Knight. London 1998.

p. 161 Maria Grazia Toderi, *Centre*, 1997. Video. Courtesy of Marconi Gallery, Milan.

p. 162 Gucci, photo Maria Vittoria Backhaus. Milan 1998.

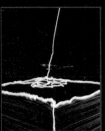
p. 163 Yohji Yamamoto, photo Satoshi Saikusa. Tokyo 1998.

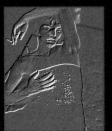
p 164 Narciso Rodriguez, photo Peter Lindbergh. New York 1998.

p. 165 Kris Ruhs, metal panels. Milan 1998.

p. 166 Mila Schön, photo Steven Klein. Dress with cuts inspired by Lucio Fontana, Milan 1961–1998.

p 167 Massimo Kaufmann, *Ubi Consistam*, 1990. Courtesy of Studio Guenzani, Milan.

captions

With thanks to the artists, the collectors, the designers, the photographers, the galleries, Lele Aquarone, Grazia D'Annunzio, Carlo Ducci, Enka Viscosa, Maria Pia Fusco, Walter Le Moli, Giò Marconi, Elisabetta Planca, G.I.E. Perles de Tahiti, Paolo Scarpellini, Roberto Silvestri, Studio Stoppini Milano, Francesca Taroni, and Vogue Italia Edizioni Condé Nast, whose contributions made this book possible.